Microsoft System Center 2012 R2 Compliance Management Cookbook

Over 40 practical recipes that will help you plan, build, implement, and enhance IT compliance policies using Microsoft Security Compliance Manager and Microsoft System Center 2012 R2

Andreas Baumgarten

Ronnie Isherwood

Susan Roesner

BIRMINGHAM - MUMBAI

Microsoft System Center 2012 R2 Compliance Management Cookbook

First published: October 2014

Production reference: 1251014

Published by Packt Publishing Ltd.
Livery Place
35 Livery Street
Birmingham B3 2PB, UK.

ISBN 978-1-78217-170-6

www.packtpub.com

Cover image by Frank (layouteam@t-online.de)

Credits

Authors

Andreas Baumgarten

Ronnie Isherwood

Susan Roesner

Reviewers

Andrew Craig

Jörgen Nilsson

Nico Sienaert

Stephan Wibier

Acquisition Editor

James Jones

Content Development Editor

Arvind Koul

Technical Editor

Dennis John

Copy Editors

Sarang Chari

Shambhavi Pai

Project Coordinator

Priyanka Goel

Proofreaders

Stephen Copestake

Maria Gould

Kevin McGowan

Indexers

Hemangini Bari

Mariammal Chettiyar

Rekha Nair

Tejal Soni

Production Coordinators

Aparna Bhagat

Nitesh Thakur

Cover Work

Aparna Bhagat

About the Authors

Andreas Baumgarten is a Microsoft MVP and works as an IT Architect with the German IT service provider H&D International Group. He has been working as an IT professional for more than 20 years. Microsoft technologies have always accompanied him, and he can also look back on more than 14 years' experience as a Microsoft Certified Trainer.

Since 2008, he has been responsible for the field of Microsoft System Center technology consulting and ever since has taken part in Microsoft System Center Service Manager 2010, 2012, and 2012 R2; additionally, he has participated in the Microsoft System Center Orchestrator 2012 and 2012 R2 Technology Adoption Program with H&D.

With his deep inside-technology know-how and his broad experience across the Microsoft System Center product family and IT management, he now designs and develops private and hybrid cloud solutions for customers all over Germany and Europe.

In October 2012, 2013, and 2014, he was awarded the Microsoft Most Valuable Professional (MVP) title for System Center Cloud and Datacenter Management.

> I would like to thank my colleague Jörg Tonn from H&D International Group for his helping hand and support with Microsoft System Center 2012 Operations Manager.
>
> The book was only possible due to the efforts of a great team. I would like to acknowledge and thank my co-authors Ronnie Isherwood and Susan Roesner.

Ronnie Isherwood, MCITP, MBCS, is a technology entrepreneur who has worked in the IT industry for more than 20 years including 15 years' experience in delivering infrastructure, systems management, and virtualization technologies to government, financial, and legal companies. He has worked with Microsoft Learning Partners as a subject matter expert and technical reviewer contributing to several MCSE courses on server and cloud. In 2014, he co-founded a software development company, JE3.COM, where he works on designing infrastructure services and software solutions for the financial services industry. Ronnie is committed to the IT community and is the founder of a Microsoft Windows user group and Chairman of BCS, The Charted Institute for IT, Jersey.

I'd like to thank Samuel Erskine for giving me this opportunity and Mélinda Isherwood for supporting me tirelessly with all my technology endeavours. I would also like to acknowledge and thank my co-authors Andreas Baumgarten and Susan Roesner for their unwavering dedication and without whom this title would not have been possible.

Susan Roesner is an IT Architect with expertise in a wide range of technologies and industries (public and private), including Fortune 500 organizations. Since 2009, she has been working in Microsoft System Center technology / IT management consulting and was responsible for Microsoft System Center Virtual Machine Manager 2010, 2012, and 2012 R2, and the Microsoft System Center Data Protection Manager 2010, 2012, 2012 R2 Technology Adoption Program, in addition to all compliance aspects within the System Center family.

Before joining H&D International Group, she worked in the finance sector and in Compliance / IT Security, working on projects such as SOX and ISMS implementations, on compliance audits (internal and external), and compliance policy/process creation.

First, I want to give a big thank you to Samuel Erskine for his great and challenging reviews that drove me toward better clarity on information I wanted to provide in the chapters. He also made it quite easy for me, as a first-time author, to understand the processes and get the job done. I also want to give thanks to Dejan Milic from H&D International Group for providing me with in-depth answers to all my questions on System Center 2012 R2 Configuration Manager.

I should also thank the team at Packt Publishing for working with us through this project. Thanks to Arvind for making sure we stuck to the schedule and to James Jones for making it so easy to work with him and for answering all my questions. Also, thanks to Stephan Wibier and Nico Sienaert, who helped make the chapters so much better with their comments and feedback.

Lastly, I want to thank my co-author, Andreas Baumgarten, who provided valuable ideas for several of the chapters and was always there when things needed to get done. Thank you to Ronnie Isherwood who took over from Samuel Erskine on such short notice to complete the last chapters and help make the book better.

About the Reviewers

Andrew Craig is a System Center Configuration Manager specialist. He has developed and delivered several Configuration Manager projects over the last 7 years in the UK and Switzerland.

He currently lives in Switzerland and works for Syliance IT Services as a senior consultant, where he actively contributes to the System Center community, speaking at community events, delivering TechNet sessions, and participating in Internet forums, such as myITForum.

Huge thanks to Samuel Erskine for introducing me to System Center back in the day in the UK and for the many adventures along the way.

Jörgen Nilsson works as a principal consultant at Onevinn AB in Sweden, working with systems management. Jörgen has over 20 years' experience in working as a consultant and is also an MCT. In 2011, he was awarded the MVP title for Enterprise Client Management. He is also an accomplished speaker and has given presentations at Microsoft Management Summit (MMS) and TechED 2014.

You can find his blog at `http://ccmexec.com`.

Nico Sienaert is 34 years old, lives in Belgium, and has more than 13 years' experience with Systems Management and related solutions. For several years, he has been working on numerous System Center implementations in Belgium and abroad.

Currently, he's working for Getronics, a world-wide system integrator, as Lead Infrastructure Consultant.

Nico is a frequent speaker on Microsoft and non-Microsoft events and writes blogs for the System Center user group in Belgium.

Microsoft awarded Nico the Microsoft MVP title for Enterprise Client Management. At this moment, he works closely with the Microsoft Product Team on Mobile Device Management.

He is the moderator of the TechNet forum for Configuration Manager MDM. Nico also works as a "virtual" employee for Microsoft as v-Technology Solutions Professional.

You can follow Nico on Twitter (@nsienaert) to stay up to date with the System Center landscape.

Nico believes that *technology never stops, and you always need to be prepared for the future*. Hence, he likes this quote from Wayne Gretzky:

> *"A good hockey player plays where the puck is. A great hockey player plays where the puck is going to be."*

> I would like to thank my daughter, Laura, and girlfriend, Kristel, for their support in pursuing this time-consuming passion of mine—IT.
>
> It was a great experience reviewing this book; I hope you like it.

Stephan Wibier is a senior consultant and an all-round IT geek, specializing in Microsoft Backend Services. He has specialized in OS deployment using tools, such as WDS/MDT and System Center Configuration Manager.

His interest in the IT business goes way back to the early '80s, starting with the good-old Commodore 64. After that, it was only a matter of time before the virus hit hard. He got certified in several areas of Microsoft products and still keeps up with the new and fabulous changes in the modern IT market.

Stephan is known for his pragmatic style, approaching problems as changes or opportunities.

www.PacktPub.com

Support files, eBooks, discount offers, and more

For support files and downloads related to your book, please visit www.PacktPub.com.

Did you know that Packt offers eBook versions of every book published, with PDF and ePub files available? You can upgrade to the eBook version at www.PacktPub.com and as a print book customer, you are entitled to a discount on the eBook copy. Get in touch with us at service@packtpub.com for more details.

At www.PacktPub.com, you can also read a collection of free technical articles, sign up for a range of free newsletters and receive exclusive discounts and offers on Packt books and eBooks.

http://PacktLib.PacktPub.com

Do you need instant solutions to your IT questions? PacktLib is Packt's online digital book library. Here, you can search, access, and read Packt's entire library of books.

Why subscribe?

- ▸ Fully searchable across every book published by Packt
- ▸ Copy and paste, print, and bookmark content
- ▸ On-demand and accessible via a web browser

Free access for Packt account holders

If you have an account with Packt at www.PacktPub.com, you can use this to access PacktLib today and view 9 entirely free books. Simply use your login credentials for immediate access.

Instant updates on new Packt books

Get notified! Find out when new books are published by following @PacktEnterprise on Twitter or the *Packt Enterprise* Facebook page.

Table of Contents

Preface

Compliance is a requirement for any company regardless of its size and configuration. Being compliant will generate benefits for your company. Take your customer purchase, sales, and invoice data as an example. Regardless of where this data resides—in an Excel sheet or Customer Relationship Management system—if the server system this data is on is stolen because it was not protected, even by a simple lock, then your company has ended up having multiple problems, and you become non-compliant. In that case:

- ▶ Your company might not be able to fulfill your customer orders or send quotes, leading to loss of revenue.

- ▶ If you are not able to regain this information, you will have a reputational issue, as customers will find out about it and not trust you any longer. In the worst-case scenario, they may cancel further work with your business.

- ▶ Your business is non-compliant because you breached data protection laws which state that sensitive data should be protected.

Being compliant will not only help you to save money in the long term and potentially keep your managers out of jail, it could also lead to competitive advantages.

In recent years, more and more companies have demanded certain certifications or adherence to standards from participants in a tender. So, being compliant with certain standards will provide you with a competitive advantage.

This book will start you on your journey to creating a compliance program and realizing the benefits of implementing this program using Microsoft Security Compliance Manager and the Microsoft System Centre family.

We will start with the basic recipes that you should have as the absolute minimum and, with each chapter, add greater complexity.

 Although throughout this book, we refer to System Center 2012, all examples have been tested on System Center 2012 R2.

What this book covers

Chapter 1, Starting the Compliance Process for Small Businesses, covers the initial recommended critical tasks to start a compliance program. It offers hands-on advice on how and where to start at a very basic level. It looks at different regulatory requirements and shows how to interpret them, how to understand the scope, and how to plan for controls.

Chapter 2, Implementing the First Steps of Basic Compliance, discusses and provides steps to start a compliance program with the free Microsoft Security Compliance Manager. Within the Microsoft environment, this tool, in addition to Best Practice Analyzer, offers tremendous help with no additional costs in starting a basic compliance program. The required steps are provided in the chapter.

Chapter 3, Enhancing the Basic Compliance Program Using Microsoft System Center 2012 Configuration Manager, provides task steps to create a GPO compliance baseline using Microsoft System Center 2012 Configuration Manager.

Chapter 4, Monitoring the Basic Compliance Program, provides task steps to monitor for breaches or adherence to your compliance program. Further recipes provide information on implementation and configuration/usage of Audit Collection Services, which is specifically designed for various compliance tasks.

Chapter 5, Starting an Enterprise Compliance Program, focuses on larger businesses that already have at least a basic IT security program in place. It is a planning chapter that provides steps leading to an enterprise-wide compliance program. It also provides explanations and examples while introducing the key steps to a successful implementation.

Chapter 6, Planning a Compliance Program in Microsoft System Center 2012, provides recipes on how to integrate the System Center products. The recipes use hands-on examples to show the required planning and implementation that must be made to align the System Center tools with the compliance process.

Chapter 7, Configuring a Compliance Program in Microsoft System Center 2012 Service Manager, is focused on recipes that aid in the creation of a compliance program using Microsoft System Center 2012 Service Manager. It provides information on how to centralize compliance information within Microsoft SCSM 2012.

Chapter 8, Automating Compliance Processes with Microsoft System Center 2012, focuses on automated centralization of control status information within the System Center family. In addition, it provides information on how to implement steps so that further automation is possible.

Chapter 9, Reporting on Compliance with System Center 2012, provides recipes on report functionalities within the System Center family. The recipes show how to create reports based on the controls created in the previous chapters.

Appendix, *Useful Websites and Community Resources*, shows that, with the System Center product family being similar to most Microsoft products, all System Center products have an extended solutions partner community. All of them have an extensive active support base on the World Wide Web. This appendix lists some of the sites that provide readymade solutions and extensive real-world dynamic content on System Center. In addition, resources are provided for compliance questions, including official (governmental) websites providing information for small businesses that want to understand their obligations, in addition to focusing resources on more technical security/compliance issues to understand the landscape that a business is working in.

What you need for this book

In order to complete all the recipes in this book, you will need a minimum of three virtual or physical servers configured with the following:

- Security Compliance Manager 3.0 and System Center 2012 R2 (or 2012) Configuration Manager
- System Center 2012 R2 (or 2012) Operations Manager with Microsoft SQL Server
- System Center 2012 R2 (or 2012) Service Manager

The following is the list of technologies the recipes depend on and their relevant versions used for this book:

- Microsoft Active Directory (Windows Server 2008 R2 and above)
- Microsoft SQL Server 2008 SP3 and above (for the System Center products)

The required software and deployment guides of the System Center 2012 R2 product can be found at the official Microsoft website at `http://www.microsoft.com/en-us/server-cloud/products/system-center-2012-r2/default.aspx`.

The authors recommend using the online Microsoft resource due to the frequency of updates to the product's requirements. Also, note that the dynamic nature of the Internet may require you to search for updated links listed in this book.

Who this book is for

The target audience of this book is administrators, security professionals, or IT managers trying trying to understand compliance capabilities. In addition, it targets compliance teams and process owners responsible for designing and implementing compliance and IT security within their businesses.

The recipes in this book start at the beginner's level and add more complexity with each chapter on compliance topics based on System Center. The ultimate goal is to provide the reader with knowledge on how to start the compliance process by understanding regulatory requirements; to enhance their existing skills in System Center with regard to compliance settings; and, most importantly, to share the experience of seasoned technology implementers.

Conventions

In this book, you will find a number of styles of text that distinguish between different kinds of information. In addition, certain terms are used within this book. As there are no universal unique meanings to them, the most important terms are explained within the next paragraph. After that, examples are provided of the styles used and an explanation of their meaning.

The following are some terms used in the book:

Terms used in book	Description
Regulatory requirement	The laws or industry standards applicable to a business and that are imposed by authorized institutes such as a government.
(Compliance) Framework	This is a set of guidelines that details an approach designed to adhere to regulations. It outlines rules to achieve this goal based on the organization's business processes and (internal) controls.
Authority document	This specifies the requirements that a company must adhere to. They may take different forms such as laws, regulations, industry best practices, customer contracts, or internal policies. It is essential that they are similar to regulatory requirements. Sometimes, certain control objectives are spelled out in them, but most often businesses have to determine those themselves.
Control objectives	Control objectives are most often abstract. They answer the questions '"what" and "why". Therefore, they can be defined by someone who understands compliance but doesn't have an in-depth technological knowledge. For example, the German data protection law specifies that transferred customer data has to be protected. So the control objective would be "data protection".
Control activities	These are activities to help ensure that requirements, stated in policies to address risks, are met. They answer the questions of "who", "where", "when", and "how." Therefore, they have to be defined by someone who has in-depth technical knowledge. Control activities may take different forms such as approvals, segregation of duties, reviews, and so on. Based on the previous example, the control activity defines who is responsible for protecting the data, which systems to include, and how data should be protected.

Terms used in book	Description
Program	A program gives a structure to compliance management. It contains authority documents and their mapping to control objectives, control activities, and documentation for the results of those controls; it might also contain risk assessments and further documentation. Quite often it is tool-assisted.
Risk management	This is the process of identifying, assessing, and managing risks. Based on company risk level, it includes the decision on whether to minimize, monitor, or control the probability and impact of those risks. Issues with negative outcomes from those risks will be transferred, minimized, or accepted.

Code words in text, database table names, folder names, filenames, file extensions, pathnames, dummy URLs, user input, and Twitter handles are shown as follows: "The provided path is the default one; please modify it for your configuration. On the destination system, start the `LocalGPO.msi` file."

Any command-line input or output is written as follows:

```
set /a x=1
:Start
net use o: \\<Name of a monitored Domain Controller\c$ /
User:Administrator hjghkgkjhgkjg
set /a x=%x%+1
if %x% NEQ 20 goto Start
```

New terms and **important words** are shown in bold. Words that you see on the screen, in menus or dialog boxes for example, appear in the text like this: "Click on the Star button next to the **Active Directory Containers** label."

Warnings or important notes appear in a box like this.

Tips and tricks appear like this.

Reader feedback

Feedback from our readers is always welcome. Let us know what you think about this book—what you liked or may have disliked. Reader feedback is important for us to develop titles that you really get the most out of.

To send us general feedback, simply send an e-mail to `feedback@packtpub.com`, and mention the book title via the subject of your message.

If there is a book that you need and would like to see us publish, please send us a note in the **SUGGEST A TITLE** form on `www.packtpub.com` or e-mail `suggest@packtpub.com`.

If there is a topic that you have expertise in and you are interested in either writing or contributing to a book, see our author guide on `www.packtpub.com/authors`.

Customer support

Now that you are the proud owner of a Packt book, we have a number of things to help you to get the most from your purchase.

Errata

Although we have taken every care to ensure the accuracy of our content, mistakes do happen. If you find a mistake in one of our books—maybe a mistake in the text or the code—we would be grateful if you would report this to us. By doing so, you can save other readers from frustration and help us improve subsequent versions of this book. If you find any errata, please report them by visiting `http://www.packtpub.com/support`, selecting your book, clicking on the **errata submission form** link, and entering the details of your errata. Once your errata are verified, your submission will be accepted and the errata will be uploaded on our website, or added to any list of existing errata, under the Errata section of that title. Any existing errata can be viewed by selecting your title from `http://www.packtpub.com/support`.

Piracy

Piracy of copyright material on the Internet is an ongoing problem across all media. At Packt, we take the protection of our copyright and licenses very seriously. If you come across any illegal copies of our works, in any form, on the Internet, please provide us with the location address or website name immediately so that we can pursue a remedy.

Please contact us at `copyright@packtpub.com` with a link to the suspected pirated material.

We appreciate your help in protecting our authors, and our ability to bring you valuable content.

Questions

You can contact us at `questions@packtpub.com` if you are having a problem with any aspect of the book, and we will do our best to address it.

1
Starting the Compliance Process for Small Businesses

This chapter covers the initial planning tasks to be worked through before you start with your compliance program. The recipes for this chapter are as follows:

- ▸ Planning the scope of the basic compliance program
- ▸ Understanding possible controls for compliance
- ▸ Evaluating the efforts of controls
- ▸ Bringing it all together into a basic compliance program

Introduction

All companies must adhere to regulatory requirements and as such, require a compliance program. For example, when a company trades, it must adhere to its local tax requirements; even a small company must have certain controls in place to ensure it remains compliant. Also, if a company accepts credit card payments, it must have controls in place to ensure it is compliant with the Payment Card Industry Data Security Standard (PCI DSS).

When creating a compliance program, it makes sense to develop processes that will benefit the business. For example, having good controls in place will simplify the audit process, lower insurance premiums, or simply protect against fines.

The purpose of the following recipes is to help you identify and plan a compliance program using System Center in conjunction with other Microsoft technologies. The examples are provided throughout the book, demonstrating how they will benefit your company.

This chapter identifies and defines the first steps in your compliance process based on regulatory standards or similar requirements and how they relate to business objectives. It provides information on how to address compliance requirements with the help of controls. It offers advice on how to interpret authority documents to extract those controls. The book specifically focuses on technical controls.

Planning the scope of a basic compliance program

Scoping is one of the keys to a successful compliance program. Irrespective of company size, you have to decide what to include and what to leave out. When scoping the requirements, take into account all the relevant business, legal, regulatory, and contractual compliance requirements. Requirements will vary from industry to industry and from country to country. Most countries have business accelerators or government agencies providing free advice; make the most of any available service to collect information for your compliance program.

Getting ready

To determine compliance requirements, different information sources can be included to assist program development during the scope-definition phase. The following list provides some potential resources:

- **Company resources**: They can include the company lawyer and internal stakeholders, such as business unit managers from the Human Resources, Finance, Operations, and Information Technology departments; they should know regulatory and contractual compliance requirements for their specific areas.

- **External resources**: They include the following:

    - **Private organizations**: This may include the Financial Accounting Standards Board, the IT Compliance Institute, or the IT Governance Institute that offer advice and information.

    - **National organizations**: They represent the industry interests and/or legal structures of a company

- **Internet resources**: Generally, they will be specific to each country; the following are some examples:

    - **US**: The Sarbanes-Oxley act is mandatory in the US and includes the regulation of financial practice and corporate governance (`http://www.soxlaw.com/index.htm`).

    - **For small business administration**: A dedicated site is available that includes all the government contacts for compliance (`http://www.sba.gov/`).

- ❑ **UK**: Companies Act 2006 (`http://www.legislation.gov.uk/ ukpga/2006/46/pdfs/ukpga_20060046_en.pdf`). More information for UK businesses including information on tax or export compliance can be found on the government website at `https://www.gov.uk/`.

- ❑ **Australia**: The following website may offer a starting point: `http://www. standards.org.au/Pages/default.aspx`.

- ❑ **Germany**: Basic information is offered by the following guide: `www.bitkom. org/files/documents/BITKOM_Leitfaden_Compliance.pdf`.

How to do it...

In order to define a scope, the following steps have to be taken:

- ▶ Understand your business compliance requirements and focus on the most critical business processes. Ask yourself the question: What is the primary product or service the business offers? Understand what is relevant to achieve any process or deliver products and/or services, for example, business units, people, applications, systems, data, and devices.

- ▶ Research the regulatory, contractual, and internal requirements using external resources and internal stakeholders.

Based on the information collected, define your *in scope* and *out of scope* objectives.

How it works...

There are two aspects to scope definition. The first aspect is, "*What company assets should you include?*" The second aspect is, "*Which regulatory requirements or standards to include in your compliance program?*"

Scope definition defined by the business

From a company perspective, the scope definition will include assets, such as physical locations, business units, equipment, application systems, and so on.

For a small or medium-sized company, defining a scope based on the compliance requirements shouldn't be a problem. Most likely, everything has to be included because data of critical applications are directly used in day-to-day business operations. In this case, separating your *in scope* part of the company and the *out of scope* part of the company might prove impossible or impractical.

Many smaller companies view compliance as a daunting task and don't start it at all. To avoid this problem, a phased approach is possible. The only consideration for a successful execution of this approach is the ability to define a self-contained scope. The benefit is that results from the first step can be incorporated into the next phase to improve on the compliance process.

For larger or more complex businesses, your decision as to what to include should be based on the following considerations:

- **Physical scope**: This includes locations or business units that have to adhere to compliance obligations.

- **Logical scope**: This includes all networks, application systems, data, and devices up to endpoint devices that use/process data that are part of the compliance obligation.

In addition, avoid situations where business units, applications, systems, or devices are both in scope and out of scope, because these could lead to breaches in your compliance program. For example, if some users are processing transaction data within an application but have limited privileges, they may be considered out of scope, whereas the IT administrator may have privileges to change data and that needs to be in scope.

That means that physical or logical separation must be possible.

Scope definition defined by regulatory, standard, contractual, or internal requirements

The other question that has to be answered for scope definition is, *"What requirements have to be met in order to be compliant?"*

Questions that should be asked are as follows:

- What are the *basic* regulatory, standard, or contractual requirements that have to be met? (This will determine which authority documents to focus on as a priority.)

- Which regulatory or standard requirements create a high risk for the business in the event of a failure?

The first question is based on the size and legal structure of a business and the industry the company is based in. The following list provides three examples of compliance areas that have to be considered:

- **Tax compliance**: Regardless of the business size, tax compliance starts with creating the business and complies with controls used in most countries that demand registration of your business and regular tax declarations. These controls will include the creation of orders and invoices that show relative tax information and the recording of payments.

- **Accounting compliance**: Just as before, regardless of size, most countries have regulatory or standard requirements demanding integrity or accuracy displayed in an annual financial statement, where the type and content depend on the size and legal structure of your company.

- **IT compliance**: As with contractual requirements, these can be in the form of software license compliance or regulatory requirements, such as data protection.

As an example of IT data protection compliance, let's look at the example from the preface, where we talked about the purchase process and systems holding customer and purchase information. To most companies, the business process that requires this information or data will be critical. Therefore, it should be considered for *in scope*.

The next question that has to be answered is, "*Which regulatory, standard, contractual, or internal requirements must be met?*" Data protection laws are one of those *basic* requirements focusing on protection of the personal data held on individuals. The financial information you hold on your customers, such as their identity information, credit card, or bank information, will fall under this category. Data protection laws vary from country to country; however, they all focus on protecting the data. Ensure that you review the respective laws; information on these laws is generally available and is easy to understand. For example, the authority document of the German protection law **Bundesdatenschutzgesetz** (**BDSG**) makes it fairly easy to understand the scope as it states in Appendix to §9 paragraph 1:

1. Prevent unauthorized access to data processing systems that process or use personalized information (physical access control)
2. Prevent unauthorized usage of data processing systems (access control)

Based on those two requirements, all locations (or just rooms), applications, networks, and devices that process, transmit, or store that information should be in scope.

The **Payment Card Industry Data Security Standard** (**PCI DSS**) is an example of *high risk* for businesses that accept, process, transmit, or store credit card data. In the event of failure in complying with PCI DSS, credit card companies, such as Visa, American Express, or MasterCard, may revoke the right to process credit card data. This could prove fatal for businesses relying on credit card payments from their customers. For those businesses, PCI DSS will definitely be *in scope* for fulfillment of an authority document.

An example on how to start with scope definition

Creating a network or architecture map is a great help in order to decide what to include to fulfill the BDSG or PCI DSS requirements. Even if you include everything in your scope, it is important to understand the relationship between your application systems, data flow, and connection points to the outside, meaning everything that is beyond your company network (for example, Internet connections). As shown in the previous example, regulatory requirements focus on specific areas. The data protection laws define certain requirements that have to be met by people (user accounts), applications, systems, and devices that handle the data. You can limit the scope of those requirements to only the relevant systems, devices, or business units.

Using a phased approach, you can start simple and then add details as you move forward with your compliance program. After the initial creation, start adding details of the systems in the network map. An important piece of information is the application used (for example, Exchange), the operating system, and the data flow of your in-scope application systems.

There's more...

You can use a degree of automation to create a network map. System Center Operations Manager is one of the tools that will help to create such a map. This will ensure that an automated diagram of your network and device landscape is created in an efficient and time-saving manner. In addition, this provides dynamic updating of your network map.

System Center Operations Manager offers different views. The **Network Vicinity Dashboard** view shows the relationship between network devices and computer (Windows Server) systems. It is a good starting point for a network map.

To view the Network Vicinity Dashboard, perform the following steps:

1. Open System Center 2012 R2 Operations Manager console.
2. Select the **Monitoring** workspace.
3. Expand the **Network Monitoring** folder.
4. Choose the device class you want to see; here, we choose **Network Devices**.
5. Go to the **Tasks** pane and click on **Network Vicinity Dashboard**.
6. The dashboard opens. Select **Show Computers** in the toolbar on top of the dashboard to view network and computer systems.

 Optionally, to change the level of connections displayed in the dashboard, change the value of **Hops** in the toolbar.

Understanding possible controls for compliance

This recipe identifies controls that may be used to fulfill compliance requirements. In addition, it maps those controls to technologies and tools such as System Center.

Getting ready

Understand your business and the scope for the compliance program based on the *Planning the scope of a compliance program* recipe.

How to do it...

Controls have two aspects to consider. On one hand, controls will provide you with a handle to fulfill compliance requirements. On the other hand, controls help you define processes and how tasks are done within the company. The most important thing to remember is *keeping it simple*. Most authority documents demand evidence of compliance but allow you to decide on the actual implementation and use of technology. Wherever possible, use automated controls based on the company's existing technologies.

The type of control implemented as part of the compliance process depends on the acceptance of your auditor, scope, the criticality of the requirement, or (simply) the budget and resources available.

The following illustration provides an overview of the type of controls:

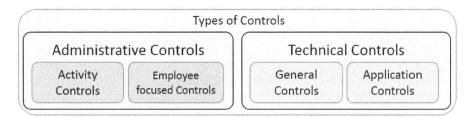

The controls are explained as follows:

- ▶ **Administrative controls**: They are most often process-related controls. For example, they influence or shape the **activity** of a process. Another example is that they reduce inefficiency and/or inconsistency.

- ▶ **Employee-focused controls**: They could include training, such as security awareness. The goal is to ensure that the employee knows what he or she is supposed to do and how.

- ▶ **Technical controls**: They focus on controls related to technical systems.

- ▶ **General controls**: They focus on the overall IT environment. The goal is to ensure that all IT operations are running in a secure and failure-free manner.

- ▶ **Application controls**: They are, as the name indicates, focused on the application level. The goal is to ensure that the processing, saving, exporting, and so on of data are correct. For example, technical controls exist to ensure the principles of orderly bookkeeping.

Regardless of compliance requirements, the implementation of administrative and technical controls is essential to ensure the survival of your company. Without any controls, the orderly conduct of business is not possible. In almost any company, some controls exist; however, they might not be obvious, as they are already integrated into the technologies used, or they may exist and not be documented.

There are also different characteristics to controls. Those include the following:

▸ **Manual controls**: They are always performed by a person.

▸ **Automated controls**: They are performed by an IT system.

▸ **Preventive controls**: They try to guard against a risk or an undesired situation from occurring.

▸ **Detective controls**: They collect data and try to discover inconsistency or whether a risk has occurred based on the collected data. Therefore, the undesired event has taken place, but it will be reported in some way to act upon.

With regard to the fulfillment of compliance requirements, the characteristic of a control must be weighted differently. For example, the most desirable control is an automated, preventive one followed by an automated detective one. Automated controls are viewed as more consistent and are not subject to personal interpretation. Therefore, an auditor will always favor those over manual ones. Keep this in mind when deciding on controls.

How it works...

The kind of control to use always depends on the situation of the company and the risk the control is supposed to address. Several factors influencing the decision of controls are listed here:

▸ The size of your company

▸ The legal structure of the company

▸ Services or products offered

▸ Employee qualifications

First, let's focus on an **administrative control**. One requirement might be to ensure the prevention of process inconsistency. The risk might be process inefficiency or an undesired activity by an employee. One example is having the right to enter supplier or customer data including financial data and the right for payment up to a certain limit. In this case, the employee could alter the bank details and then issue a payment; alternatively, the employee could split a payment into two if the bill is higher than his or her allowed payment limit.

The most desired control would be an **automated preventive** one. In this example, a role-based access control would prevent the first example, as most modern purchase order systems allow the creation of roles and tying those to certain rights or areas. The preventive measure here provides segregation of duty by splitting the process between two employees, preventing risk.

An **automated detective** control could be to check whether bank information for a certain supplier or customer has been changed right before a payment. To mitigate the second example, check if several payments have been made within a short timeframe with the same reference number.

When focusing on small companies, segregation of duties might not be possible, or the application might not offer role-based access controls. In this case, a **manual preventive** control could be used. One example is the four-eye principle. In this case, another employee has to approve payment as well.

The least desirable control would be **manual detective**. The amount of data or the number of transactions due to automated IT systems has been growing so much that inconsistency will most likely not be visible. Nonetheless, a manual detective control could be to pick several payments and check them for orderly processing.

Administrative controls have a protective function, as they try to prevent undesired events from happening. They do not exist to monitor every movement of an employee. Instead, they try to mitigate the risk that an employee might face a situation where, under pressure, an undesirable event could occur.

The next example focuses on **technical controls**. Again, we will use the purchase order system as an example. As mentioned before, data protection laws require protection of sensitive data. As an example, the German BDSG mentioned in the first recipe requires access control to prevent unauthorized usage. Please refer to *Appendix, Useful Websites and Community Resources*, for further information on BDSG.

The standard PCI DSS is fairly general, it demands access control in the form of authentication or logon without mentioning any system. As part of an authentication procedure, most companies will use a username and password combination. The kind of authentication procedure might depend on the product or service offered.

For highly sensitive products such as the ones in the military, research, or the medical industry, a more sophisticated implementation might be desirable. This will shape the kind of control required. We will focus on the most common authentication with a username and password. In order to ensure a meaningful password, many companies have an administrative control in place requiring adherence to a password policy.

An automated preventive control is the introduction of Microsoft Active Directory and the creation of a **Group Policy Objects** (**GPO**) that demands a certain password complexity. Therefore, a user will be prevented from using shorter, non-compliant passwords. The same thing might be possible within applications.

An automated detective control could be a tool that scans for undesired passwords. In this case, employees could use a non-compliant password, but the administrator would receive a report showing these. The administrator is now in a situation to remediate instances of non-compliance or recommend further action in the case of repeated occurrence.

A manual preventive control could be the usage of password letters. In this case, an employee would create passwords.

A manual detective control isn't feasible to ensure complexity of passwords. However, an example can be ensuring that only relevant people have access to an application. In this case, HR would provide a list of employees who have left the company or changed positions. The compliance team with the IT team would check whether those employees are no longer active in critical applications.

To understand the kind of controls available, you can try using a brainstorm technique. This could include the following:

 ▸ Talking to application owners to identify existing application controls, for example, roles in an application for an access management control

 ▸ Researching industry best practices for the objective you have; for example, access (and identity) management offers many papers from Microsoft on how to achieve this using Microsoft **Active Directory Domain Service** (**AD DS**)

 ▸ Researching frameworks that offer a list of controls

Evaluating the efforts of controls

The following recipes provide information on how to evaluate controls based on the benefit they have for your business.

Getting ready

Understanding the controls considered and the one-time cost and operational cost associated with them.

How to do it...

When identifying and deciding on the controls, bear in mind the principle *keep it simple*. Most authority documents only require evidence of compliance but do not demand certain controls. Therefore, use controls that are available within your company whenever possible. When brainstorming for possible controls for a given requirement, use the most efficient and cost-effective one. Many times, one control might not be sufficient, and several controls may have to be implemented to get the desired effect.

The most straightforward approach is to look at the objective and answer the question whether the control will reduce the risk of reaching your objective within an acceptable level. An acceptable level could mean that some controls will not reach their goal. To do this, a matrix is a great help.

A more holistic approach is harder to evaluate, as the cost of a control is most often easier to calculate than the benefit it creates. Still, it should be considered. When deciding on the right control, do not only look at the control itself but at the broader scope the control has on your business. It is important to understand what technology could be used to implement this control or what technology is underlying the control and could be used to create benefits to the business. The following illustration provides some examples on cost versus benefit for controls that help evaluate which controls to choose:

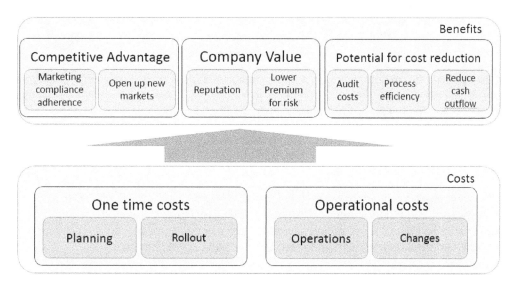

Automated controls are always more desirable than manual ones. The cost effectiveness of such controls comes from the following:

▶ Automation of monitoring and regulation activities

▶ Achievement of a much higher coverage through automated controls, for example, an example eliminating a higher percentage of (fraud) risks

▶ Creating process efficiency

▶ Creation of objective controls as they lower audit costs

In the previous recipes, we talked about compliance requirements for access and authentication management. In the next recipe, we will discuss authorization.

Access and identity management is a compliance requirement that is found in different regulatory requirements. In cases where identity lifecycle management is purely a manual activity, creating controls for this might may seem like creating more manual work; however, by introducing Microsoft Active Directory Domain Services, the identity lifecycle management process, including deletion and changes, will be more efficient.

GPO for password compliance is an automated control already within the AD DS. The only manual effort is deciding on GPO and configuring it within AD DS. The overall one-time cost of planning an Active Directory Domain and implementing it will outweigh the cost and resources required for manual activities, such as using creation and management in each and every application as well as ensuring password compliance to meet requirements. Hence, the potential exists to create more efficient processes within systems and applications.

Audit costs are quite often lower for automated controls than for manual ones. Automated controls do not face the risk of human error or subjective interpretation. Therefore, auditors require more evidence that a manual control is effective, thus qualifying for the goal of the control.

Another qualifier for an automated control is a detective one, as those could help to minimize undesirable cash outflow. Think about an example; suppose that the wrong supplier has been chosen, leading to the loss of favorable supplier conditions, such as discounts.

The competitive advantage should be considered to evaluate the usage of a control. Controls help prevent failure of the company or a certain unit. As an example, take PCI DSS and the result of noncompliance.

Creating a compliance program could open up new markets, while noncompliance could eliminate them. The PCI DSS mentioned in the previous recipe is an example of eliminating a customer base in the case of noncompliance. As mentioned before, without compliance, the credit institutes reserve the right to revoke processing of credit cards.

Another competitive benefit of compliance controls is opening up new customers and markets. One of the most basic compliance regulations, tax compliance, is such an example. In many countries, governmental bidding invitations are only open to companies that have declared tax in time and have paid their taxes. The consequence of noncompliance could be the loss of potential orders.

More companies demand certain IT security certification to be eligible to provide a bid. As IT security is one of the aspects of many regulatory requirements, the first step toward such a certificate is already made.

How it works...

Evaluating the effectiveness of a control requires research on your part to understand the impact they have on the business. At one side are the costs incurred by them, and on the other side are the possible benefits when implementing them.

Bringing it all together into a basic compliance program

This recipe provides advice and examples on how to read an authority document and extract the requirements it contains. In addition, the recipe will provide examples on how to translate those requirements into controls.

Getting ready

Obtain the authority documents that you want to focus on. Most of them are available on the Internet.

Work through the previous recipes *Planning the scope of a compliance program* and *Understanding possible controls for compliance*.

How to do it...

The key is to understand the authority documents. The first step is to extract the required control objectives or the goal(s) and, based on the required evidence or activities, to define the control activities. After identifying and defining the control objectives and control activities, the next step is to relate those to the actual implementation within the business. The process looks as shown in the following illustration:

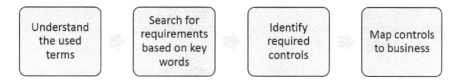

Step 1 – understanding the terms of the authority document

Understanding the terms of the authority document is essential as each authority document might put a different meaning on key terms. Sometimes, the authority documents contain explanations of such key terms. Quite often, there are accompanying documents that offer more detailed explanations.

For example, the German BDSG defines key terms in §1 to §3. In addition, the **Federal Commissioner for Data Protection and Freedom of Information** (**FfDF**) provides the document *BDSG – Text and Explanations* that comments not only on key terms but also on objectives and required controls.

Step 2 – identifying objects and/or requirements based on key words

The next step in creating your compliance program is to *identify objectives and/or requirements based on keywords* within the authority document. Examples of such keywords are **control**, **monitor**, **prevent**, **protect**, **identify**, and so on. Note those paragraphs as they are the input for the next step. In addition, if authority documents are updated or changed, you know the origin of a certain control objective or control activity. Knowing the originals will make it much easier to incorporate updates or changes into your compliance program.

For example, the German BDSG is quite clear on objectives. As mentioned before, Appendix (to §9 paragraph 1) states the following:

> *3. to ensure that people authorized to use a data processing system can only access data they are authorized for, ...(access control),*

This example is easy to understand as the keyword, **access control**, already states the control objective or goal. *Ensuring access management* is the control objective we have to look at.

Step 3 – identifying controls that fulfill this objective

The next step in our process is to *identify controls that fulfill this objective*. In order to do this, the following two questions should be answered:

▸ What is necessary for a risk *not* to occur?

▸ What reasonable steps and control(s) do we have to implement to reach the goal?

Going back to the example from step 2, the *risk* addressed is unauthorized access. Therefore, the authority documents focus on the *authorization mechanism*. The controls have to ensure the risk is limited and/or mitigated.

Implement the correct scope that is relevant to the effort required to implement each control.

Step 4 – mapping controls to your business – defining the scope

Based on the authority document, we know that sensitive personal data is included; thus, with regard to our purchase order system, all sensitive data within it will be in **scope**. We also know, based on the previous example, that any person with access to this information within the application must be included. The focus here is on the *digital* person, meaning their technical identity, such as user *accounts*.

Step 5 – mapping controls to your business – defining the type of controls

Depending on your company and environment, different controls could be used. Thinking back on the type of control, an *application control* such as *automated preventive* is most desirable. A sophisticated approach is to use a **role-based access control**. This requires an application system that provides capabilities to create roles with rights to access certain information or functions and to actually configure and use those capabilities. In this case, the application itself will automatically prevent users from accessing information they are not authorized for. Looking at our example of a purchase order system, most applications already provide such functions and role concepts. They just have to be configured. The benefit of using such a control is quite high, while the cost incurred is quite low.

Some applications do not offer such role-based access controls. In this case, a manual preventive control could be used to ensure *basic* authorization control. A possible control is an approval process. Before a system administrator grants access to the application, the line manager and information owner have to authorize access to the application and data for that given user. The prerequisite is that an authorization mechanism is configured for the application.

Step 6 – mapping controls to your business – defining the broader scope to simplify controls

The last step is to understand those controls in the broader scope—that of the business. BDSG will not be the only authority document requesting controls in access management. Look at the broader scope and evaluate whether a more generalized approach is more appropriate. Creating either the automated or manual control will benefit the company, as it will minimize the risk of fraud. The authority document states that people authorized to use the application are in scope as well as the application.

While evaluating the controls, the implementation of role-based access control or access management controls might be more expensive and time-consuming at the first view. However, considering that most likely not only one application but many applications have to have access management (authorization) controls, it might be more cost-effective to consider the broader scope using a role-based access management solution. To manage those access rights consistently and efficiently, they should not be configured individually. Instead, access rights should be given on a group level, most likely standing for a certain role those people have. Each role or group allows the fulfillment of a certain aspect of a job, such as managing purchase orders or approving purchase orders. So, all rights required to manage purchase orders, such as creating, changing, or deleting orders, will be included. The usage of those roles will have the added benefit of making the access and identity management process much more efficient for administrators.

The following table provides further examples on control objectives and possible technical implementations for controls with regard to the authority document:

Authority document	Authority document goal	Technology to achieve goal	Scope	Cost/benefit
PCI DSS – 7.1 Limits access to system components and cardholder data to only those individuals whose job requires such access	Ensures access management	Segregation of duty within the application and OS Use of automation, such as **System Center Orchestrator** (**SCO**), to grant access based on roles	All accounts/ applications with access to cardholder data	**Cost**: Planning and implementation of segregation of duty **Benefit**: Process enhancement, for example, automated provision of accounts Reduces risk of fraud
Sarbenes Oxley Act (SOX) – Section 404 Demands annual report on adequate internal control for financial reporting	Several goals, for example, monitoring	Audit trails or logs of applications use SCOM ACS for monitoring	All critical applications with financial transactions (criticality must be defined by business)	**Cost**: Planning and implementation of SCOM ACS **Benefit**: Reputation

Many authority documents will not provide clear and detailed information on the goals and how to realize them. The preceding categories should guide you in how to take them apart to determine control objectives, subsequently control activities, and determine what Microsoft technologies to use to achieve them.

How it works...

The compliance program you create and manage will help to ensure adherence to compliance requirements. The results of the compliance program are only as good as your understanding of the authority document and implemented controls. A thorough planning phase is very important.

Adopt the steps described previously according to your specific requirements and company.

Prioritize your authority document and control implementation. For example, you could create a matrix for high risks, putting in all regulations or standards that have a high impact on your business. As shown in previous recipes, if you depend on credit card payments from customers, fulfillment of the PCI DSS standard is essential to your continuous business operations. So this should receive high risk.

Export compliance is essential to any international freight shipping business; otherwise, it might be considered low priority. It has to be considered but not in the first phase.

Likewise, consider controls that are easy to implement and cover a large number of requirements. There are many more examples, so look at the authority documents, and understand how they impact your business and which controls will fulfill those requirements.

2
Implementing the First Steps of Basic Compliance

In this chapter, we will cover the following topics:

- ▸ Preparing for the creation of a compliance baseline
- ▸ Installing Security Compliance Manager
- ▸ Creating a compliance baseline using GPO to ensure system security
- ▸ Implementing the GPO Baseline into Active Directory

Introduction

Our compliance process starts with a simple tool called **Microsoft Security Compliance Manager**. This free tool allows you to create and centrally manage compliance baselines based on **Group Policy Objects** (**GPOs**). The tool is used to compare your GPOs against established standards and to export them for use within other configuration management tools. The focus of Security Compliance Manager is on technical compliance. It includes industry best-practice baselines and supports auditing existing baselines. Security Compliance Manager allows you to kick-start your compliance program for existing technologies such as **Active Directory Domain Services**.

You could buy one of the compliance tools that offer more functionality and cover a broader spectrum of compliance; however, before spending the money, it is worth reviewing this free tool that may cover your requirements. Start with a technology that is already available within your environment and use or enhance this to create your compliance process. Only start to think about adding more complexity to your compliance process *after* you have mastered the recipes shown in this chapter. Think of it like building a house. First, you have to build the walls and roof and add windows and doors. Only *after* you have completed those steps do you have a basis from which you are able to add complexity—such as electricity or interior design—without having to worry about damage to your house or theft.

Preparing for the creation of a compliance baseline

This recipe provides information on activities that should be performed before creating a compliance baseline and installing Security Compliance Manager.

Getting ready

In order to create a meaningful and successful basic compliance program, it is essential that a clear understanding of your goals exists. As mentioned in *Chapter 1*, *Starting the Compliance Process for Small Businesses*, you have to define what you want to achieve with your compliance program. The creation of the compliance baseline using Security Compliance Manager will affect part of your company or all of your company's users and/or systems, as it is based on the domain policy. For example, if you introduce a stricter password policy, all the appropriate stakeholders must be involved.

How to do it...

To create a compliance baseline based on the Active Directory domain policy, the following areas have to be researched and/or prepared:

- Technical aspects:
    - Understand the Active Directory and Domain Policies; two very good sources are the TechNet sites `http://technet.microsoft.com/en-us/library/hh147307%28v=ws.10%29.aspx` and `http://technet.microsoft.com/en-US/windowsserver/bb310732.aspx`.
    - Create an Active Directory group that will include all users that require administrative access; this will be used to allow access to Security Compliance Manager to create baselines, edit baselines, run audits, and so on.

▶ Role and responsibility aspects:

❑ Decide on the users that will form the administrator/operator group. Add them to the Active Directory group mentioned previously, and place this group in the local administrator group on the Security Compliance Manager system. No other user should have access to this system.

❑ Your stakeholders must be involved in the process of creating baselines. These baselines will affect most or all of your company's users and, sometimes, systems. It is therefore essential for successful implementation that management is involved in the process. Earlier, we mentioned the password policy, but another example could be enforcing saving Microsoft Office documents to departmental shares by default or enforcing saving documents in a newer Office version. Not involving management may lead to questions and support incidents being raised. In addition, you should involve the application owner if your company has this role. Based on your results from *Chapter 1*, *Starting the Compliance Process for Small Businesses*, different baselines may be required for more sensitive data and/or systems including user accounts.

How it works...

Security Compliance Manager uses GPOs to implement settings such as user rights and define computer behavior and so on based on the configuration within your baseline. As certain users (groups) or computers (groups) have different requirements, different baselines may be required. In order to create a baseline to secure your environment, you should familiarize yourself with the following:

▶ OU design
▶ GPO design

OU design

An **organizational Unit** (**OU**) is a container within Active Directory Domain Services that allows you to structure objects, such as users, computers, groups, and printers. These objects are used to manage, secure, and potentially segregate the administration of your company environment. It is like the walls within your house creating separate rooms for different purposes. You might have users that are only working with very sensitive data, whereas other users don't. So, you might consider having stronger security requirements for the first group. To do this, you create a separate OU container for each set of users. When designing OUs, keep it as simple as possible and refer to best practices before starting. Microsoft provides a video containing best practices that can be viewed by visiting the following link:

```
http://channel9.msdn.com/Events/TechEd/NorthAmerica/2012/WSV206
```

If you do not have an OU design yet, the following are the design considerations. The term *level* describes how deep we are within the AD structure. So, a possible approach could be the following:

- ▶ **Level 1**: **OU for Computer** contains all computers such as client systems.

- ▶ **Level 1**: **OU for Server** contains all server objects.

- ▶ **Level 1**: **OU for User** contains all users.

- ▶ **Level 1**: **OU for Group** contains all groups.

  Depending on your requirements, you might need more OUs on this level, for example, one for service accounts.

- ▶ **Optional Level 2**: Under **Server**, you can create additional OUs that define the server type, allowing further segregation, such as an **OU for Hyper-V** and an **OU for Webserver**. A reason to do this could be if you have requirements, for example, if you need to harden web servers, but not your other servers, you create the OUs below **Server**. This should only be done if you want to create baselines just for those server types.

- ▶ **Optional Level 2**: Under **User** you can create additional OUs for stricter security settings. For example, **OU for Department XX** could be created in case people have access to sensitive data and require a higher security level. As mentioned before, only create these OUs if you require them and want to create settings/rights that require an additional OU. Sometimes, sensitive user accounts do not belong to just one department. In this case, Security groups may be a better solution.

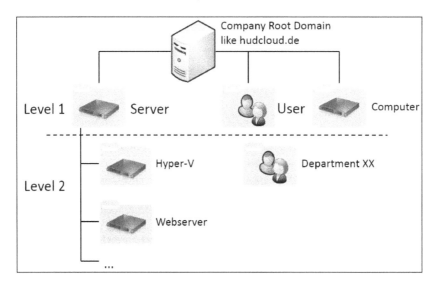

GPO design

GPOs are used to administer and enforce settings at domain or OU level. This allows you to ensure a consistent configuration across all users and computers within your company. Using GPOs is a good way to enforce compliance; by grouping objects together, you avoid the need to manually enforce settings on specific computers.

It is quite important to understand that there is an order of precedence for GPOs. It is possible to have more than one GPO for the same object. A local group policy object that is applied to a computer or user may not take effect if a domain-linked GPO targets the same object. This is because the later GPO overrides the local group policy. Further information can be found at `http://technet.microsoft.com/en-us/library/cc785665(v=ws.10).aspx#feedback`.

If your company does not have any GPO policies yet, the following are general considerations:

- **Creating a Domain Policy**: This one will affect your whole company, including all systems and users within your domain
- **Creating a Server Policy**: This will affect only your servers and could be used for basic settings, such as remote desktops or updates
- **Creating a Client Policy**: This will be for client computer systems
- **Creating a Client User Policy**: This will be for your users

 Additional GPO policies can be created as required.

The following diagram shows where those policies could be applied within your OU design:

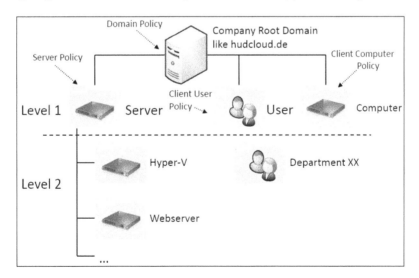

Installing Security Compliance Manager

This recipe shows the steps required for a successful installation of Security Compliance Manager.

Getting ready

You should prepare a physical or virtual system to install Security Compliance Manager on. In addition, you should complete the previous recipe *Preparing for the creation of a compliance baseline* before starting the installation.

How to do it...

The prerequisites for installing Security Compliance Manager are as follows:

- Prepare an account that has administrative privileges on the system where Security Compliance Manager will be installed

- Ensure you have access to Group Policy Management Console and read-access to AD

- Ensure you have a compatible operating system; at the time of writing, a client system with Windows 7, Windows 8 and later, or a server system with Windows 2008 R2 or Windows 2012, is sufficient

- Install the prerequisites as follows:

    - Windows Installer 4.5 (already included in Windows 8 and Windows 2012).

    - Microsoft .NET Framework 4; ensure that .NET Framework 3.5 is installed on the system. If you do not preinstall it, the installation will fail on Windows 8, Windows 2012, and later. You will have to provide an installation source, such as a Windows 2012 DVD (`<Drive letter>:\Sources\SxS`) when installing it on Windows Server 2012. The following screenshot shows the place to enter the path:

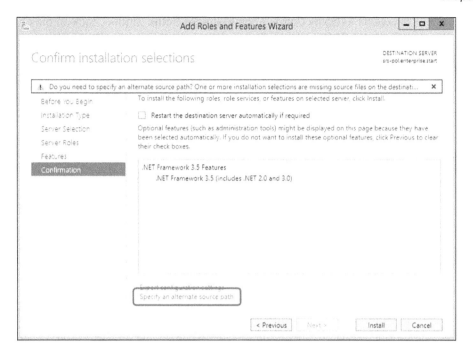

 Optionally, install a local instance of SQL server 2008 or higher; otherwise, a SQL Server 2008 Express edition will be installed automatically.

> ▶ Download the Security Compliance Manager from `http://www.microsoft.com/en-us/download/details.aspx?id=16776`

> ▶ In case no other SQL server is installed, download SQL Server 2008 Express Service Pack 3 from `http://www.microsoft.com/en-us/download/details.aspx?id=27594`

To install Security Compliance Manager, perform the following steps:

1. Go to your downloaded source file and run `Security_Compliance_Manager_Setup.exe` as administrator.

2. Accept the **User Account Control** asking for permission for the installation.

3. In the next two steps, all prerequisites are installed, including the following:

   ❏ The Microsoft Visual C++ 2010 x86 redistributable—accept the license terms, click on **Install** to start the installation, and then click on **Finish** to complete it

   ❏ .NET Framework 3.5 (only if not previously installed—please refer to the prerequisites in the case of an error)

4. In the **Microsoft Security Compliance Manager Setup** window, click on the checkbox **Always check for SCM and baseline updates** and click on the **Next** button.

5. Accept the licensing terms, and click on the **Next** button.

6. In the next window, either accept the default path C:\Program Files\Security Compliance Manager, or click on the **Browse** button and change to a customized path. After that, click on the **Next** button.

7. In the window **Microsoft SQL Server 2008 Express**, click on the **Next** button to install the database.

8. Accept the licensing terms in the next window for Microsoft SQL Server 2008 Express and click on the **Next** button.

9. The **Ready to install** window shows the installation summary. Click on the **Install** button to start the installation.

10. On Windows 8 and Windows Server 2012, an error message appears for the SQL installation. Accept this by clicking on **Run the program without getting help**. This window (shown in the following screenshot) is expected and does not influence the installation process. For a stable environment, SQL 2008 Express SP3 must be installed after the installation.

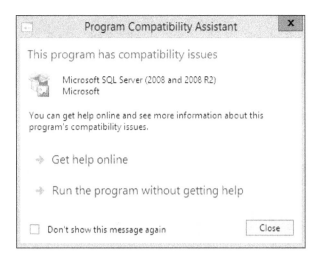

11. The next window shows the successful installation of Security Compliance Manager. Click on the **Finish** button to complete the installation.

12. The **Microsoft Security Compliance Manager Console** opens, and an automatic download of baselines starts:

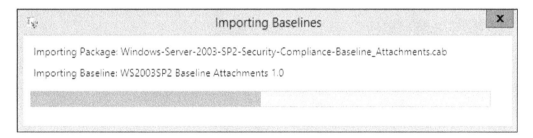

13. Before doing anything else, close the console, go to the SQL Server 2008 Express Service Pack 3 download, and install it for all components.

How it works...

The installation of Security Compliance Manager is fairly simple. The important part is to ensure all prerequisites are met. There are no special hardware requirements, as a normal provisioned client system with Windows 7 or Windows 8 and later, or a server system with Windows 2008 R2 or Windows 2012, is sufficient. At the time of writing, these are the currently supported Windows versions.

If no database existed prior to the installation, a SQL 2008 Express database will be created. This stores the established standards and custom baselines in addition to audits and reports.

See also

For further details on the installation process, please go to the TechNet site at `http://social.technet.microsoft.com/wiki/contents/articles/1866.microsoft-security-compliance-manager-scm-getting-started.aspx`.

For further details on the compatibility of SQL server, please go to `http://blogs.msdn.com/b/psssql/archive/2012/09/01/installing-sql-server-on-windows-8.aspx`.

Creating a compliance baseline using GPO to ensure system security

This recipe provides an introduction to basic compliance, focusing on small businesses.

Getting ready

You should read the previous two recipes *Preparing for the creation of a compliance baseline* in addition to *Installing Security Compliance Manager*.

How to do it...

Research the subject by doing one or more of the following things:

▶ Research the settings available in group policies, including the product-specific ones you can download. Understand the settings and the risk they mitigate. Information for most group policies is available on the Internet, or you can even use Security Compliance Manager itself as it shows policy information. Additionally, there are tools that help you create your own policies for application and system settings.

▶ Based on your organizational requirements, corporate policies, and compliance standards, along with any regulatory requirements, define your compliance baselines and determine which OUs the baselines should target.

To create a compliance baseline, perform the following steps:

1. Open Security Compliance Manager. If updates for compliance baselines are available, an update window, similar to the one shown in the following screenshot, will appear; select all the baselines you require:

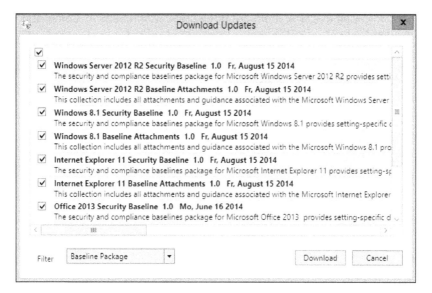

2. In the next window, agree to add all the baselines you downloaded, and click on **Next**.

3. Click on **Import** to make all baselines available in Security Compliance Manager. Have a look at the following screenshot:

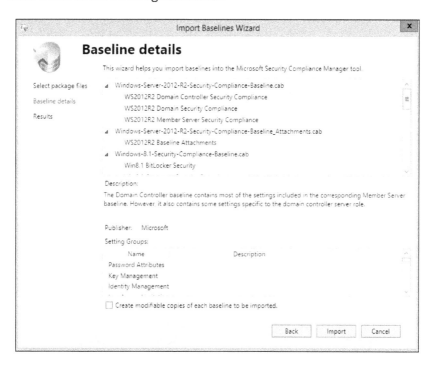

As shown in the following diagram, there are three areas within Security Compliance Manager Console:

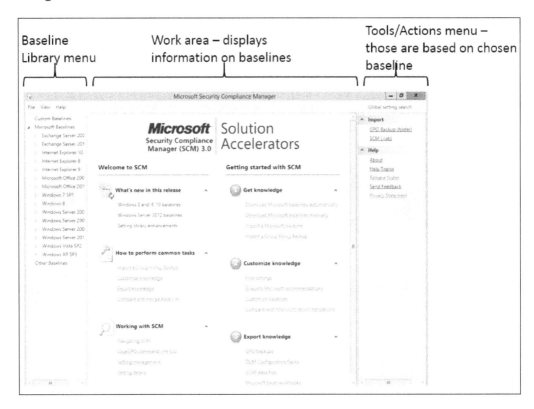

The following table provides information on the functions of those three areas:

Navigation area	Description
Baseline Library	In this navigation menu, you will find all GPO baselines that were imported. Under **Microsoft Baselines**, the automatically imported baselines are shown.
	Those baselines are write-protected and cannot be changed. They are a best-practice approach. In order to always have these best-practice GPO baselines available, they should remain write-protected.
	All baselines that can be changed can be found Under **Customized Baselines**.
Work area	This area displays information on the SCM or on the baselines/settings you selected in Baseline Library.
Tools/Action	This navigation menu displays available actions or tools that are usable. The available actions depend on your Baseline Library of choice.

The most important features of Security Compliance Manager are as follows:

▸ Creation of new GPO-based baselines

▸ Creation of baselines based on an existing one (copy of an existing baseline)

▸ Checking (and optionally merging) an existing GPO against an industry best-practice

▸ Exporting created baselines for use in other tools

▸ Testing created baselines against Active Directory

The easiest way to create a compliance baseline is as shown in the following screenshot:

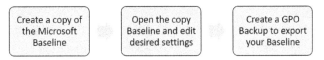

As discussed in the preface and *Chapter 1, Starting the Compliance Process for Small Businesses*, securing your systems is essential for a successful compliance program. Access management is part of several regulatory requirements, such as privacy laws, PCI DSS and SOX. As usernames and passwords are one of the easiest access controls to implement, we will start our compliance program with a simple control to ensure adherence to a password policy.

1. Within Security Compliance Manager, go to **Microsoft Baselines** and open, for example, the Windows 8.1 folder. There are several compliance baselines available depending on which kind of settings/configuration/rights you want to customize. As we want to create a password policy, we have to select the **Domain Security Computer** policy. Have a look at the following screenshot:

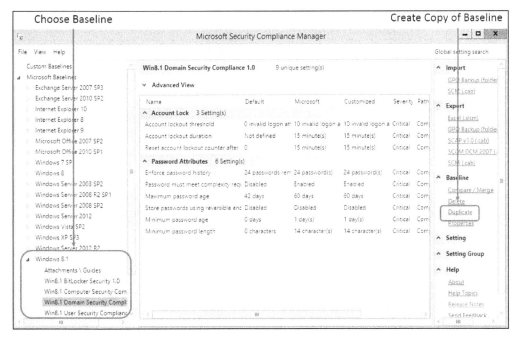

2. From the **Actions** menu, select **Duplicate**. Click on the **Baseline Name** field, enter a name for your custom baseline, for example `HuDCloud Domain Security Compliance`, and then click on **Save**. This will create a copy of the baseline.

3. The custom baseline you created should launch automatically; it is displayed in the console under **Custom Baselines**.

4. Click on this baseline. In the work area, you will find all settings that are available within it.

   The first column displays the name of each settings group; under each settings group is the name of each individual setting. For example:

   ❑ The **Default** column shows the default value of the setting.

   ❑ The **Microsoft** column shows the Microsoft-recommended setting.

   ❑ The **Customized** column shows the value of the setting if it has been modified.

   ❑ The **Severity** column provides a severity level for this setting with regard to securing your environment. The following table gives a brief description of the severity levels:

Severity	Description
Critical	Settings with the severity level **Critical** should be configured when implementing a security- or compliance-related baseline. This rating means that not configuring the setting is considered high-risk and could have a serious impact on the security of your environment, system, or data. Microsoft recommends *every company* to consider configuring all settings with **Critical** severity.
Important	Settings with the severity level **Important** have a significant impact on computers or data stored and should be considered for computers with sensitive data.
Optional/None	Settings with the severity level **Optional** have little or no impact on security, and **None**, similarly, is unlikely to affect security; however, this does not mean they should not be applied subject to the settings and requirements in your company.

   You can change the severity level on custom baselines. When designing a custom baseline, be careful not to change the severity level unless there is a clearly documented reason; otherwise, when reviewing a baseline, a critical setting could be overlooked.

5. Each baseline comes with relative information about its settings. To access this information, select a baseline in the **Baseline Library** menu, and then navigate to **Attachments | Guides**. For example, for Windows 8.1, you can access the `Windows 8.1 Security Guide.docx` as shown in the following screenshot:

6. To create your password policy baseline, you must configure the settings values based on your security and compliance requirements. As shown in the next screenshot, make the following changes:

    1. Navigate to **Customized Baselines** and then open the **HuDCloud Domain Security Compliance** baseline.

    2. In the work area, select (for example) **Minimum password length** and, in the **Customize setting value** field, enter your required value. Each value that you customize is shown in bold characters afterwards:

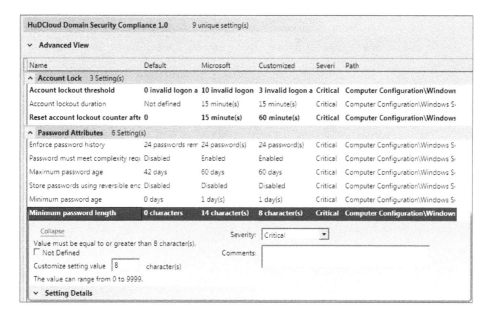

7. When designing security and compliance baselines, it is paramount for success that you understand each setting in detail. It is best not to make an educated guess, as detailed settings information is just a click away. To access this information, click on **Setting Details**. A small example of the details available for the password complexity setting is as follows:

    ❑ The meaning of minimum password length and full information about the minimum complexity requirements, such as uppercase and lowercase characters and digits.

- ❏ The kind of **vulnerability** this setting eliminates or mitigates.

- ❏ The **impact** that this setting has; a section of the detailed information that aligns with this chapter is that, if you enable the password complexity setting, an increased level of helpdesk request may be logged, as there would be more than the usual number of password lockouts. Earlier in the chapter, we mentioned the need to involve management in the creation of compliance baselines; for this setting, by involving management, a strategy can be provided for users to create and remember more complex passwords before the deployment of the policy is initiated.

- ❏ **Countermeasure** details; this advises on mitigating risk and may suggest combining a setting with other settings to achieve compliance and/or enhanced security. Have a look at the following screenshot:

8. After you are satisfied with your changes, you need to export the customized baseline. To do this, go to the **Actions/Tools** menu and, under the **Export** section, click on **GPO_Backup (folder)**. The **Browse for folder** dialog will open; select the folder that you want to export your GPO to. After the export, a folder with the exported GPO will open containing the backup.

You are now ready to enforce your first compliance baseline based on GPO settings.

How it works...

Creation of a new compliance baseline is made easy by the folks at Microsoft, who have compiled and provide information based on established standards for GPOs. These standards included severity levels and recommended setting values for the most common computer, user, and application settings. Each baseline contains detailed information on each setting; valuable help is provided to customize it based on company requirements.

> Use the information provided in the baseline as a starting point. Even though established standards are provided, careful considerations have to be made when selecting settings. What works in one company may not work in another company. In addition, some of the settings may not be up-to-date with the latest research on recommended configuration.

There's more...

As mentioned before, Security Compliance Manager offers more functionality. Some useful functions are discussed in the next sections.

Auditing or checking your existing GPO policies against established standards

If you already have a GPO policy within your company, there is an option to check your policy against the industry best practice as shown in the baselines provided by Microsoft. The following steps show you how to do this and assume you have access to, and are familiar with, **Group Policy Management Console** (**GPMC**):

1. Open **Group Policy Management Console**, navigate to your domain, and then expand the tree until you see the GPO that you want to compare with.

2. Right-click on your GPO and then select **Back up**, as shown in the following screenshot:

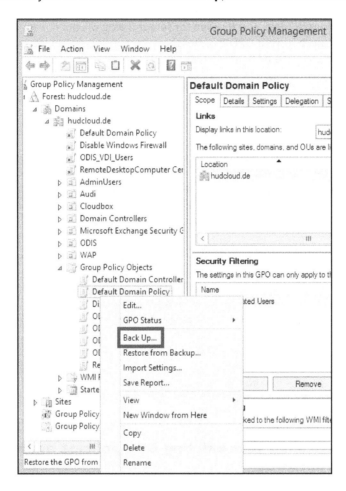

3. Enter a backup folder and then click on **OK**.

4. Copy the GPO export created to the system where Security Compliance Manager is installed.

5. Open **Security Compliance Manager Console** and, in the **Action/Tools** menu under **Import**, choose **GPO_Backup (folder)**. In the new window, go to the folder you copied your company GPO to and import it. The **GPO Name** dialog opens and the GPO name is displayed by default. If required, you can change the name by clicking on the **Baseline Name** field and entering an alternative name. To accept the default name or a modified name, click on **OK**.

6. The **SCM Log** dialog opens displaying the status of the import. Click on **OK** to close the dialog. The imported baseline is now listed under the **GPO Imports** section under **Custom Baselines**.

7. In the **Baseline Library** menu, select a customized baseline, here we will select the previously created baseline **HuDCloud Domain Security Compliance**. If you do not have one, create it before proceeding. This baseline will be used to merge your existing GPO policy. The customized baseline you choose should contain all your changes.

8. In the **Action/Tools** menu, select **Compare/Merge**:

9. A new window opens asking you for the GPO policy that the Security Compliance Manager should compare against. Choose your company baseline. Have a look at the following screenshot:

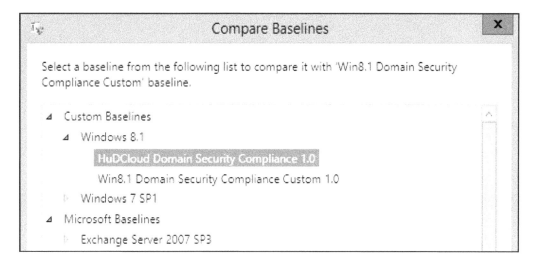

10. As shown in the preceding screenshot, a summary is shown with a number of the same, and different, settings. Click on **Close** to finish your review. Have a look at the following screenshot:

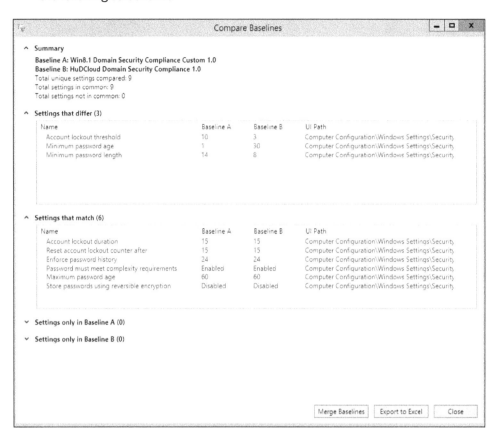

 Optionally, notice the **Merge Baselines** button; this feature allows you to merge two baselines. You may want to merge two similar custom baselines to reduce management complexity during a department merger.

11. In case you want to merge two baselines, click on the **Merge Baselines** button to start the process. In the new window, you have to decide which setting to use for each setting that differs between your two policies. Check the radio button beside each value, and click on the **OK** button. This will start the merge process:

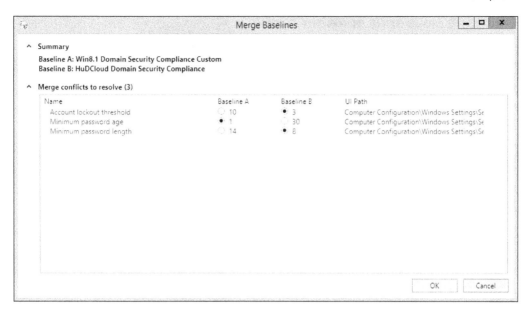

12. The **Export to Excel** button will create a useful spreadsheet; this contains the following four workbooks:

   ❑ Differences

   ❑ Matches

   ❑ Settings only in A

   ❑ Settings only in B

13. This spreadsheet is useful to share information with auditors or managers, to anyone who does not have access to the Security Compliance Manager console, or to record information at a point in time.

14. After the merge, you will be able to export the compliance baseline based on the GPO and import it into your Active Directory. Please see the next recipe for the process.

When designing and importing baselines in SCM, it is important to know that not all GPO settings are supported; for example, group policy preferences are not supported. To find out more about what is, and is not, supported, you can review the SCM FAQs; these can be viewed at
`http://social.technet.microsoft.com/wiki/contents/`
`articles/1836.microsoft-security-compliance-`
`manager-scm-frequently-asked-questions-faq.aspx#Q_`
`What_setting_types_are_not_supported_i.`

Exporting baselines to other tools

The Security Compliance Manager tool is great for testing and configuring GPO-based compliance. System Center Configuration Manager offers more compliance functionalities, but it lacks the testing capabilities and out-of-the-box baselines the Security Compliance Managers offers. Therefore, it makes sense to create and test your baselines with SCO. Then use System Center Configuration Manager for operations as you are able to centralize more compliance controls within this tool. The following steps provide a guideline to the export of your GPO-based baseline. For more details on System Center 2012 R2 Configuration Manager, please refer to *Chapter 3, Enhancing the Basic Compliance Program Using Microsoft System Center 2012 Configuration Manager*.

1. Open the Security Compliance Manager Console.

2. In the **Baseline Library** menu, choose the baseline you want to export.

3. In the **Actions/Tools** menu, expand **Export**. As shown in the following screenshot, several options are available. For usage in other configuration tools, such as System Center Configuration Manager, choose the `.cab` format. Here simply select **SCCM_ DCM_2007 (.cab)**:

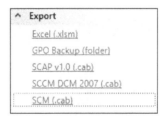

4. In the file explorer window, choose your export folder; under **File name:** choose a name for your CAB file and then select **Save**. You are now ready to import the baseline to another tool.

Deploying new GPO settings

So far, we talked about Security Compliance Manager and GPOs with regard to compliance management. The tool also enables you to deploy baselines based on industry standards for new technologies. For example, in June and September 2014, new Security Compliance Manager baselines were provided by Microsoft for Windows 8.1, Windows Server 2012 R2, and Microsoft Office 2013. Hundreds of new GPO settings are made available with those new technologies. Security Compliance Manager helps to test those new settings and decide which settings to use.

The following link provides information about new baselines as they are made available:

```
http://blogs.technet.com/b/secguide/archive/2014/09/04/scm-baselines-
for-windows-8-1-ie-11-and-server-2012-r2-are-now-live.aspx
```

Active Directory Domain Services fine-grained password policies

Since Windows 2008 R2 AD DS, fine-grained password policies have been available. With those policies, you are able to create different policies for different groups of users. For more information, please see the following URL:

```
http://technet.microsoft.com/en-us/library/056a73ef-5c9e-44d7-acc1-
4f0bade6cd75.aspx
```

Implementing the GPO baseline in Active Directory

This recipe provides information on how to implement the created baselines from the previous chapter into your company Active Directory.

Getting ready

The previous recipes should be finished before proceeding with this one.

How to do it...

The overall process of starting with the second recipe *Preparing for the creation of a compliance baseline*, moving to the third recipe *Creating a compliance baseline to ensure system security,* and finishing with this recipe is summarized in the following diagram:

Create an Organizational Unit design for your environment	⇨	Use the SCM tool to create the GPO's for your environment	⇨	Use the GPMC to link and manage the GPOs

To use the created GPO Baseline and implement it into your company's AD, open the GPMC console and navigate to the GPO where you want to import the GPO baseline settings. If you have not already created a GPO, you will need to do so. Be aware that the password policy is different from other policies, because it has to be applied to the default domain policy unless the AD DS fine-grained password policy is used. Refer to the *There's more...* section for further details.

In order to implement the Password GPO baseline, perform the following steps:

1. Open the **Group Policy Object Editor** and navigate to **Computer Configuration | Windows Settings | Security Settings | Account Policies | Password Policies**.

2. Right-click on the **GPO** and choose **Import Settings**.

3. The **Import Settings Wizard** opens, click on **Next**. On the **Backup GPO** page, click on **Backup** to create a backup of your current GPO to be on the safe side (for restore options).

4. On the **Backup Group Policy Object** page, click on the **Location** field to choose a backup folder and optionally provide a description, and then click on the **Back Up** button.

5. After a successful backup, you will automatically return to the **Import Settings Wizard**. Click on **Next**.

6. Click on **Browse** to choose the folder of your customized GPO that you want to import. Click on **Next**.

7. Under **Backed up GPOs**, all available GPO's are visible. Select the correct one and click on **Next**, as shown in the following screenshot:

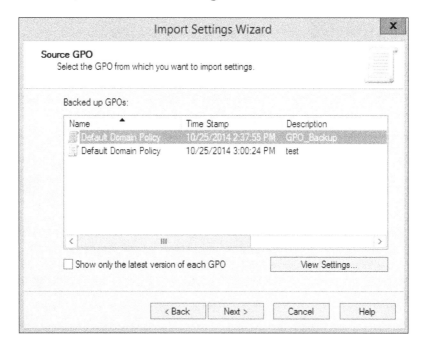

8. On the **Scanning Backup** page click on **Next**.

9. On the **Migrating References** page, select **Copying them identically from the source** and click on **Next**, as shown in the following screenshot:

10. A summary window appears. Click on **Finish** to start the import.

 It is essential to thoroughly test your OU and GPO designs before deploying them in a production environment.

There's more...

Before importing your customized GPO baseline into your company GPO, you should perform extensive testing. Depending on the kind of settings you made, protocols, applications, or rights may no longer be available.

Test your customized GPO baseline using LocalGPO

With LocalGPO, you can do the following:

▸ Apply a security baseline to the local group policy of a computer

▸ Export the local group policy of a computer to a group policy backup

▸ Create a GPOPack to apply the same settings to a computer without installing LocalGPO

▸ Test multiple group policies

LocalGPO is part of the Security Compliance Manager Setup package. It is not installed automatically. To install it on your test system, go to the Security Compliance Manager system, copy the installer file `LocalGPO.msi` that is in the path `C:\Program Files (x86)\Microsoft Security Compliance Manager\LGPO` to your destination system. The provided path is the default one, please modify it for your configuration. On the destination system, start the `LocalGPO.msi` file. Agree to the license agreement, and click on the features to be installed. Follow the wizard to the **Install** page to finish it.

You are now ready to test your GPO baseline on a local computer. Copy the GPO baseline that you created with Security Compliance Manager to your system. Remember to export the baseline first, following step 8 from the recipe *Creating a compliance baseline using GPO to ensure system security*. To apply the GPO policy to your test system, the following steps have to be performed:

1. Log on to the test system using an administrator account.

2. Go to the LocalGPO folder under applications and right-click on the command-line tool. Choose **Run as administrator** to open the tool. At the time of writing, the LocalGPO version included with SCM 3.0 does work up to Windows 8 and Windows Server 2012.

3. At the command prompt, type `cscript LocalGPO.wsf /Path:<path to your customized baseline>`.

4. Press the *Enter* key to finish the import.

5. Now test the settings that you changed, and make sure that all features, applications, and user actions are still possible.

If you want to revert to the original local GPO policy, perform steps 1 and 2, and enter the command `cscript LocalGPO.wsf /Restore`.

The Advanced Group Policy Management tool

The **Advanced Group Policy Management** (**AGPM**) tool provides additional functionality to work with group policy. Some of the features include:

▶ Backup and restore group policy

▶ Change control for the implementation and acceptance of change to policies

▶ E-mail notification of policy edits

▶ An audit trail and history of edits from which you can roll back to earlier versions of a policy as well as the means to comment on changes, allowing other administrators to quickly understand a change

You can find out more about the AGMP tool at `http://www.microsoft.com/en-us/windows/enterprise/products-and-technologies/mdop/agpm.aspx`.

3
Enhancing the Basic Compliance Program Using Microsoft System Center 2012 Configuration Manager

In this chapter, we will cover the following topics:

- ▶ Configuring Microsoft System Center 2012 Configuration Manager for compliance
- ▶ Creating a baseline to monitor for unapproved software
- ▶ Creating a baseline to monitor for unapproved hardware and virtual systems
- ▶ Using Security Compliance Manager baselines in Microsoft System Center 2012 Configuration Manager

Introduction

In this chapter, we will expand upon our basic compliance program by implementing and monitoring compliance with Microsoft System Center 2012 Configuration Manager (Configuration Manager).

Configuration Manager can be used to implement compliance for Windows servers, desktops, laptops, and Windows mobile devices, as well as devices that run Mac OS, Android, and iOS operating systems.

Configuration Manager has most of its compliance features under an application section named *Compliance Settings*. Prior to Configuration Manager 2012, Compliance Settings was known as **Desired Configuration Management** (**DCM**).

In this chapter, we will focus on creating Configuration Items, baselines, and compliance rules.

The prerequisites for all recipes in this chapter are as follows:

- An installation of Microsoft System Center Configuration Manager 2012. The SP1 and R2 versions are also suitable.

- The reporting point site system role must be installed and configured.

- A Windows Active Directory domain with at least one member server. This should be a test server.

- An installation of Microsoft Security compliance manager.

Configuring Microsoft System Center 2012 Configuration Manager for compliance

Configuration Manager can monitor compliance by assessing the status of client configuration settings. These configuration settings are created by the administrator or by importing settings created by a software vendor. You assign compliance rules to the settings and then create and deploy baselines used to assess the compliance status of a given collection (a group of devices).

The types of setting you can configure are as follows:

- Active Directory Query
- Assembly
- File System
- IIS Metabase
- Registry Key
- Registry Value
- Script
- SQL Query
- WQL Query
- XPath Query

Each setting type list has options and, in some cases, sub setting types. For example, the File System setting allows you to work with files or folders and can be used to assess values and/ or conditions, such as file presence or folder permissions, date modified, version number, and any filesystem details.

This recipe shows you the steps required to configure Configuration Manager for compliance.

The scenario for this recipe will be that a line of business application requires a local license file to be present on a server; it must also have specific permissions granted to that file.

The recipe will include the following steps:

1. Creating a group and assigning access to Configuration Manager Compliance Settings.
2. Creating a configuration item.
3. Creating a configuration baseline.
4. Deploying a configuration baseline.
5. Monitoring and reviewing baseline compliance.

Getting ready

Before starting, you will require the following:

▶ An installation of Configuration Manager 2012 with at least one agent deployed to a Windows 2012 Server or a Windows 8 Desktop

▶ A collection that includes the Windows 2012 server or Windows 8 desktop

▶ A user account that is assigned the **Compliance Settings Manager** role or the Configuration Manager **Full Administrator** role

▶ Clients should be enabled for compliance evaluation

▶ The Configuration Manager **Reporting services point** site system role must be installed and configured

How to do it...

Perform the following steps to create a group and assign access to Configuration Manager Compliance Settings:

1. Create a group in Active Directory called `Compliance Administrators`.
2. Assign only those users whom you allow to create and review compliance in the Configuration Manager console.
3. Use a Configuration Manager administrative account and launch the **Configuration Manager Console**.

4. In the **Configuration Manager Console**, on the left-hand side, click on **Administration**, click on the arrow to expand the **Security** node, click on **Administrative Users**, right-click on a blank area of the page, and then click on **Add User or Group**.

5. Click on **Browse**, in the **Enter the object name to select** field, type Compliance Administrators, and then click on **OK**.

6. Click on **Add**, click on the checkbox next to **Compliance Settings Manager**, and then click on **OK**.

> In Configuration Manager, you can specify which scopes, collections, administrative users, or groups are assigned allowing granular control of compliance settings for different departments and systems. This is particularly useful if certain compliance areas address more sensitive data.

Creating a configuration item

Perform the following steps to create a configuration item:

1. In the **Configuration Manager Console**, click on **Assets and Compliance**, and then click on the arrow to expand **Compliance Settings**.

2. Right-click on **Configuration Items**, and click on **Create Configuration Item**; the **Create Configuration Item Wizard** launches.

3. On the **General** page, click on the **Name** field, and then type LOB application licence file check.

4. Click on the **Description** field, and then type a description. In the type of configuration item section, leave the default (**Windows**).

5. Click on the **Categories** field, and the **Manage Administrative Categories** window opens. Click on the checkbox next to the items **Server** and **Line of Business**, click on **OK**, and then click on **Next**. Have a look at the following screenshot:

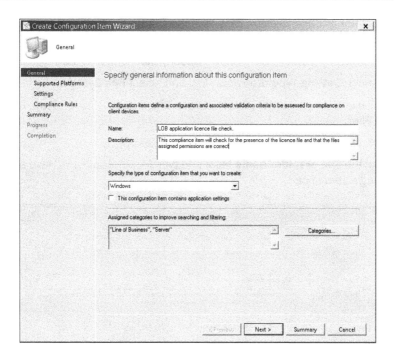

6. On the **Supported Platforms** page, leave all the default operating systems selected for assessment, and then click on **Next**. Have a look at the following screenshot:

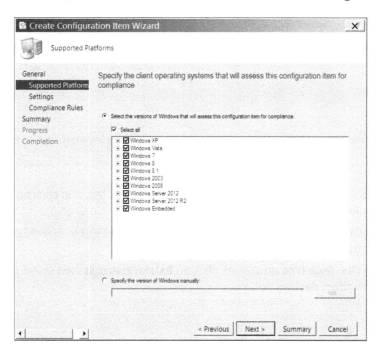

7. On the Settings page, click on **New**, and the **Create Settings** page opens.

8. On the **Create Settings** page, click on the **Name** field, and type `LOB application licence file check`. Click on the **Description** field, and then type a description.

9. Click on the **Setting Type** drop-down list, and select **File System**.

10. In the file and (lower section) folder section of the page, click on **Type**, and then select **File**.

11. Click on the **Path** field, and then type `c:\mylobapp`.

12. Click on the **File or folder name** field, and type `mylobapp.txt`. Have a look at the following screenshot:

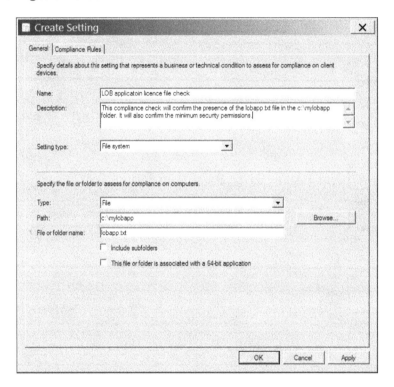

13. At the top of the page, click on the **Compliance Rules** tab, and click on **New**; the **Create Rule** page opens.

14. On the **Create Rule** page, click on the **Name** field, type `File check`, click on the **Description** field, and then type a description.

15. Click on the **Rule type** dropdown, click on **Existential**, and then select the **File must exist on client devices** option.

16. At the bottom of the page, click on the **Noncompliance severity for reports** drop-down list, select **Critical**, and then click on **OK**. Have a look at the following screenshot:

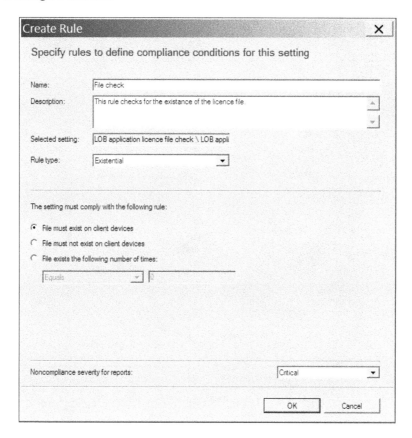

17. On the **Create Settings** page, click on **New** to create an additional rule.

18. On the **Create Rule** page, click on the **Name** field, type `Check file permissions`, click on the **Description** field, and then type a description.

19. Click on the **Rule Type** drop-down list, and select **Value**.

20. Click on the **Property** drop-down list, and then select **Permissions**. Click on **Exclusive**, and then click on **Add**. The **Enter user group** page is launched.

Note that you will need to enter a service account with sufficient access to evaluate the files and permissions. The account used in the book is for demonstration purposes; you will need to use a test account created in your own domain.

21. Type `hudcloud.de\mylobapp_svc`, and then click on **OK**.

22. Click on the **Noncompliance severity for reports** drop-down list, select **Warning**, click on **OK**, and then click on **OK** again. Have a look at the following screenshot:

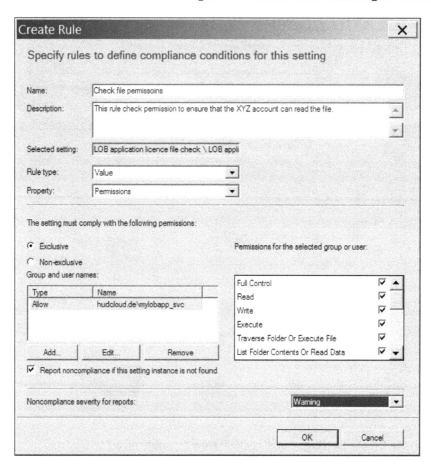

23. On the **Settings** page, click on **Next**; on the **Compliance Rules** page, click on **Next**; on the **Summary** page, review the details, and click on **Next**:. Have a look at the following screenshot:

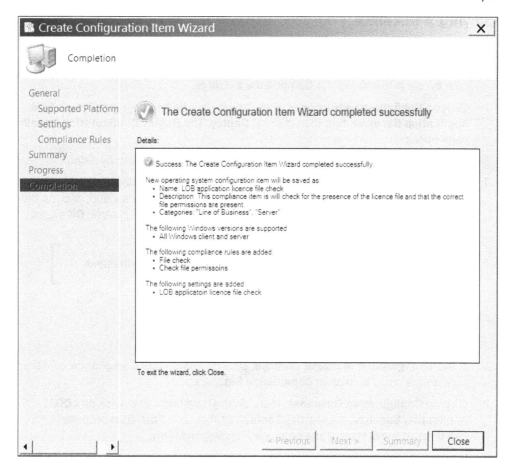

24. Click on **Close**.

Creating a baseline

Perform the following steps to create a baseline:

1. In the **Configuration Manager Console**, click on **Assets and Compliance**, and then click on the arrow to expand **Compliance Settings**.

2. Right-click on **Configuration Baselines**, and click on **Create Configuration Baseline**; the **Create Configuration Baseline** page is launched.

3. Click on the **Name** field, and type LOB Application Baseline; click on the Description field, and type a description.

4. In the **Configuration data** area, click on **Add**, and then click on **Configuration Items**.

5. Under **Available configuration** items, click to highlight **LOB application licence file check**, click on **Add**, click on **OK**, and then click on **OK** again.

Deploying a baseline

Perform the following steps to deploy a baseline:

1. In the **Configuration Manager Console**, click on **Assets and Compliance**, and then click on the arrow to expand **Compliance Settings**.

2. Click on **Configuration Baselines**, then on the right-hand side, right-click on **LOB Application Baseline**, and then click on **Deploy**. The **Deploy Configuration Baselines** page opens.

3. The **LOB Application Baseline** configuration baseline is selected by default.

4. In the **Collections** section, click on **Browse**; on the **Select Collection** page, click on the dropdown, and select **Device Collections**; in the **Name** section, click on the collection that contains your test server, click on **OK**, and then click on **OK** again.

 Note that baselines can also be targeted to **User Collections**.

Monitoring and reviewing baseline compliance

Perform the following steps to monitor and review baseline compliance:

1. In the **Configuration Manager Console**, click on **Assets and Compliance**, and then click on the arrow to expand **Compliance Settings**.

2. Click on **Configuration Baselines**, then, on the right-hand side, click on **LOB Application Baseline**. Review the **General**, **Status**, and **Statistics** sections and then, at the bottom of the page, click on **Deployments**.

3. Review the status, right-click on the headings, and review what additional information you can add to the screen. Notice that under the **Action** heading, the current status has the value **Monitor**.

4. In the lower part of the screen, right-click on the **LOB Compliance Baseline**, and then click on **Properties**.

5. Click on the checkbox next to **Remediate non-compliance rules when supported**.

6. Click on the checkbox next to **Generate and alert:**, click on the **When compliance is below** field, and change the value to **80**%. Click on **OK**.

7. Notice that the **Action** status has changed to **Remediate**.

How it works...

Compliance baselines in Configuration Manager require that you create Configuration Items and rules and then assign them to a baseline. The baseline can be deployed to a collection. You can configure notification and then carry out remediation tasks manually or automatically. Note that automatic remediation is only available on script-, registry-, or WMI-based CIs and only when using an equals operator.

For example, you can right-click on the baseline and select to create a new collection of devices from all the non-compliant devices. You can then deploy software or configuration changes to only those non-compliant clients.

There's more...

The following sections outline additional compliance functionality that, while outside the scope of this chapter, may be related to your company's compliance requirements.

Compliance assessment scheduling

Compliance Settings are, by default, evaluated every 7 days. You can amend this using the followings steps:

1. In the **Configuration Manager Console**, click on **Administration**, click on **Client Settings**, highlight the **Client Settings** item on the right-hand side (for example, **Default Client Settings**), and then, on the menu at the top, click on **Properties**. The **Default Settings** window is launched.

2. On the left-hand side, click on **Compliance Settings**, and then, under **Device Settings**, click on **Schedule**. You can implement a simple schedule by updating the evaluation frequency values in minutes, hours, or days. Alternatively, you can create a customized schedule.

Remediation

For items that support it, you can configure automatic remediation; in large organizations or for some critical or sensitive settings, this may be preferred.

User data and profiles

Configuration Manager is a user and device configuration management and inventory tool; you can associate users with multiple devices, including assigning a primary device. You can configure compliance settings to control folder redirection, offline files, and roaming profiles on computers running Windows 8 and above. You can build compliance so that these features work differently based on the primary and any other device. For example, you could enable offline files only on a user's primary device.

Company Resource Access

Company Resource Access allows you to create profiles that are user-specific, including certificates, VPN, and Wi-Fi profiles.

 Company Resource Access settings do not appear for Configuration Manager admins who are assigned the Compliance Settings Manager role. They must be assigned the **Company Resource Access Manager** role.

Remote Connection Profiles

Remote Connection Profiles allow users to remotely connect computers from the Internet or other domains.

See also

▶ http://technet.microsoft.com/en-us/library/gg682154.aspx

Creating a baseline to monitor for unapproved software

This recipe provides the steps required to create a baseline that can be used to monitor for unapproved software.

Configuration Manager has the ability to inventory clients for a list of all installed software. The inventory includes the following details.

Configuration item	Description
Software category	Software categories allow you to define and group software at a high level. There are almost 100 prepopulated categories to help you get started; you can also create a category of your own. Some examples of existing categories are **Line of Business** and **Purchasing**.
Software family	Software families allow you to define and group software more specifically; for example, if the category is **Line of Business**, then the family could be **Payroll** or **CRM**.
Software label	Software labels allow you to define specific attributes that can be used to group software for reporting purposes. You can assign up to three labels for software; for example, you could create labels such as Authorized and/or Maintained. You can then assign these to all approved software that have a maintenance contract.

The following illustration shows the properties of inventoried software to which we have assigned a **Category** and a **Family** from the preconfigured items. Have a look at the following screenshot:

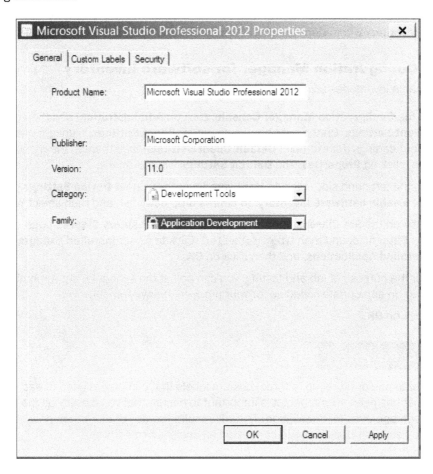

You can monitor and report on software more easily when the inventoried items have been assigned categories and families. In addition, the creation and assignment of custom labels allows you to quickly identify unclassified and, more importantly, unauthorized software installations.

This recipe will include the following steps:

1. Enabling Configuration Manager for software inventory.

2. Creating software labels.

3. Assigning software labels.

4. Reporting unapproved software.

Getting ready

Before you can scan for unapproved software, you must inventory the installed software and then categorize it. You must first enable the software installation inventory feature of **Hardware Inventory** within **Configuration Manager Client Settings**.

Enable Configuration Manager for software inventory

You can enable inventories using the following steps:

1. In the **Configuration Manager Console**, click on **Administration**, and then click on **Client Settings**. On the right-hand side, under **Client Settings**, highlight one of the client settings (for example, **Default Client Settings**), and then on the menu at the top, click on **Properties**. The **Default Settings** window opens.

2. On the left-hand side, click on **Hardware Inventory**, under **Device Settings** click on the **Enable hardware inventory on clients** drop-down list, and then select **Yes**.

3. Click on the **Set Classes** button; on the **Hardware Inventory Classes** page, click on the **Filter** field, and then type Installed. Click to select **Installed Executable** and **Installed Applications**, and then click on **OK**.

4. For the purpose of lab and testing, you can adjust the schedule, but remember to plan an appropriate schedule for your production environment.

5. Click on **OK**.

How to do it...

You can create one or more (up to three) custom labels that can be assigned to each item of software that has been inventoried. It is important to ensure that you classify all the software that has been approved for installation. This will require the use of more than one label. Once all software has been classified, you can report on unclassified software.

Creating a software label

Perform the following steps to create a software label:

1. In the **Configuration Manager Console**, click on **Assets and Compliance**, click to expand **Asset Intelligence**, and then click on **Catalog**.

2. On the ribbon at the top of the screen, click on **Create Software Label**, the **Create Custom Label Wizard** is launched.

3. Click on the **Name** field, and type `Approved`. Click on the **Description** field, type `This software has been approved for installation on the corporate desktop PC's`, click on **Next**, then again on **Next**, and then click on **Close**. Have a look at the following screenshot:

Assigning a software label

Perform the following steps to assign a software label:

1. In the **Configuration Manager Console**, click on **Assets and Compliance**, click to expand **Asset Intelligence**, and then click on **Inventoried Software**.

2. For the purpose of this example, we will click on **Microsoft Security Compliance Manager**; however, you can click on any software. Right-click on it, and then click on **Properties**.

3. Click on **Custom Labels**, click on the drop-down list next to **Label 1**, select **Approved**, and then click on **OK**.

Reporting unapproved software

Perform the following steps to report unapproved software:

1. In the **Configuration Manager Console**, click on **Monitoring**, click to expand **Reporting**, then click to expand **Reports**, and then click on **Asset Intelligence**. Have a look at the following screenshot:

2. Click on the **Search** field, type `Label`, and press the *Enter* key. Right-click on **Software 12A – Software titles without a custom label** and click on **Run**.

3. Click on **Values**, click on the **Collection** that contains the servers or desktops you require for the report, and then click on **OK**.

4. Click on **View Report**.

When you have assigned custom labels to all installed software, you can report on unlabeled (unapproved) software.

How it works...

In Configuration Manager, by enabling **Hardware Inventory**, you can inventory software on all discovered devices running the Configuration Manager agent. When discovery data has been collected, the installed software is listed in the **Asset Intelligence** section, where you can manually add labels to software. The labels you create help to define and report on what is and isn't authorized software. By scheduling inventories to run periodically, you can monitor and notify the staff of unapproved software installations and take appropriate action accordingly.

There's more...

As well as running ad hoc reports, you can create subscriptions that automate notifications. You can do this by right-clicking on the report and then clicking on **Create Subscription**. You can then schedule reports to be created in a specific file path or to be sent via e-mail.

See also

The term software inventory may seem confusing, but in the case of Configuration Manager, it refers to another inventory task that is not the same as the hardware inventory of installed software (which queries WMI). Software inventory is the scan of client disks for files, folders, and executables. You can read more about it using the following link:

`http://technet.microsoft.com/en-us/library/gg682126.aspx`

Creating a baseline to monitor for unapproved hardware and virtual systems

Configuration Manager can monitor for unapproved systems that have been deployed to a corporate network. It does this by running periodic discoveries from one or more of the available discovery methods. These methods are listed in the following table:

Discovery method	Description
Active Directory Forest Discovery	Allows Configuration Manager to discover Active Directory sites and subnets.
Active Directory Group Discovery	Allows Configuration Manager to discover the group membership of Active Directory users and computers.
Active Directory System Discovery	Allows Configuration Manager to discover computers in Active Directory Domain Services.
Active Directory User Discovery	Allows Configuration Manager to discover user accounts in Active Directory Domain Services.

Discovery method	Description
Heartbeat Discovery	Allows you to specify the frequency with which Configuration Manager clients send a heartbeat discovery record to the site.
Network Discovery	Allows Configuration Manager to discover network resources by scanning domains, SNMP devices, and DHCP servers. The following are the three discovery types: ▸ **Topology**: Finds the network topology by scanning IP subnets and routers with a definable number of hops. ▸ **Topology and client**: Finds the network topology and potential client devices. ▸ **Topology, client, and client operating system**: Finds the network topology, potential client devices, and their operating systems and versions.

The recipe will include the following steps:

1. Enabling a discovery method.
2. Reviewing discovered data.

Getting ready

When deploying Configuration Manager, by default, only the Heartbeat Discovery method is enabled. You must plan and enable the discovery method you will use and the frequency of ongoing discovery.

How to do it...

For this recipe, you can use an Active Directory System Discovery in a controlled lab environment. Ensure that only the required lab servers are discovered by placing them in a designated test **Organizational Unit** (**OU**).

Enabling a discovery method

The following steps show you how to discover devices in a specified OU. In this recipe, we will use the Active Directory System Discovery.

1. In the **Configuration Manager Console**, click on **Administration**, click to expand **Overview**, click to expand **Hierarchy Configuration**, and then click on **Discovery Methods**.

2. Right-click on **Active Directory System Discovery**, click on **Properties**, and then click on the checkbox next to **Enable Active Directory System Discovery**.

3. Click on the Star button next to the **Active Directory Containers** label. The **Active Directory Containers** page opens.

4. Click on the **Browse** button next to the **Path** field, navigate to and select your test **OU**, click on **OK**, and then click on **OK** again.

5. Click on the **Polling Schedule** tab, and then click on **Schedule**. On the **Custom Schedule** page, click on **None**, click on **OK**, and then click on **OK** again.

6. Right-click on **Active Directory System Discovery**, and then click on **Run Full Discovery Now**. On the next screen, select **Yes** to confirm that you want to run a full discovery as soon as possible.

Reviewing discovery data

You can use a Configuration Manager query to quickly view devices not running a Configuration Manager client.

In the **Configuration Manager Console**, click on **Monitoring**, click on **Queries** and, in the center of the page, right-click on **All Non-Client Systems**, and then click on **Run**.

The query returns all discovered devices that don't have the Configuration Manager client installed or have had the client removed.

How it works...

After you have enabled a discovery method and configured the discovery target and intervals, Configuration Manager collects and stores data found about devices and potential clients in the Configuration Manager database. You can then query the database for information on discovered records.

There's more...

Each discovery method has a number of options used to reduce the impact on system performance during discovery. You review each discovery method and test and document them in your lab before planning a production deployment.

Delta Discovery

Delta Discovery works by only discovering objects in Active Directory that are new or have changed since the time of the last discovery.

Delta Discovery can be used to reduce performance impact on the Configuration Manager site server that allows you to increase the discovery frequency. Delta Discovery works with Active Directory users, groups, and systems.

See also

▶   The *Planning for Discovery in Configuration Manager* article at `http://technet.microsoft.com/en-us/library/gg712308.aspx`

Using Security Compliance Manager baselines in Microsoft System Center 2012 Configuration Manager

Configuration Manager has the ability to import the Security Compliance Manager GPO settings. Using these imported settings, you can audit, notify, and report on machine and device compliance. This is particularly useful for security administrators who wish to know that the policies defined are in place across an organization.

For example, if an administrator has overridden a policy manually on a Windows desktop, or if administrators have blocked group policy inheritance for an organizational unit, there would be no way of knowing about it unless it were reported by a user or technician.

The Configuration Manager agent can report on whether the desired compliance settings are in place so that when you have implemented domain-wide or other group policy settings, you can validate that they are deployed and take action based on the information reported in Configuration Manager.

The recipe then shows how to create a baseline that uses the imported Configuration Items to monitor for password compliance.

Getting ready

Before you start this recipe, you must have successfully completed all of the recipes in Chapter 2, *Implementing the First Steps of Basic Compliance*.

How to do it...

Perform the following steps to export the Microsoft Security Compliance Manager baseline:

1.   Launch the Microsoft Security Compliance Manager Console; on the left-hand side, click on the baseline you want to export. For the purposes of this guide, click on the **+** sign next to **Windows 8.1**, and then click on **HuDCloud Domain Security Compliance 1.0**.

2. Wait for the baseline to load; then, on the right-hand side, under **Export**, click on **Configuration Manager DCM 2007 (.cab)**. You will get a screen similar to the following screenshot:

3. If required, you can change the name here; otherwise, keep the default name, browse to the location you will store the file in, and then click on **Save**.

 If any setting can't be exported to the Configuration Manager CAB file format, an additional dialog box will advise you of this. You can then browse and correct any incompatible settings; in addition, an error log will be stored in the same location as the .cab file.

To import the Configuration Manager DCM CAB file, perform the following steps:

1. In the **Configuration Manager Console**, click on **Assets and Compliance**, and then click on the arrow to expand **Compliance Settings**.

2. Click on **Configuration Items**; then, on the ribbon at the top, click on **Import Configuration Data**; the **Import Configuration Data Wizard** is launched.

3. On the **Select Files** page, click on **Add**, navigate to the .cab file you created earlier, click on the file, and then click on **Open**. If you are prompted that the publisher of the .cab file could not be verified, click on **Yes**, and then click on **Next**.

4.   On the **Summary** page, review the details, click on **Next**, and then click on **Close**:

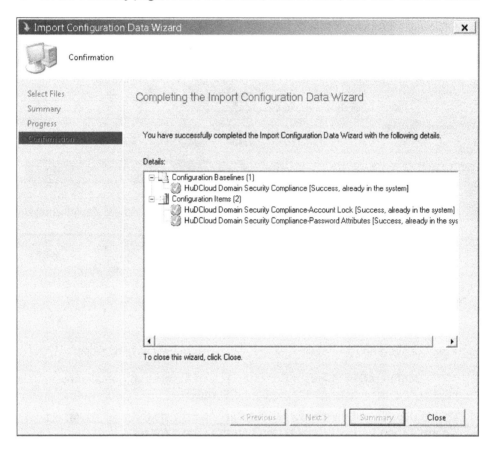

To create a baseline to monitor password compliance using the new Configuration Items, perform the following steps:

1.   In the **Configuration Manager Console**, click on **Assets and Compliance**, and then click on the arrow to expand **Compliance Settings**.

2.   Right-click on **Configuration Baselines** and click on **Create Configuration Baseline**; the **Create Configuration Baseline** page is launched.

3.   Click on the **Name** field, and type WS2012 Domain Security Compliance; click on the Description field, and type a description.

4.   In the **Configuration data** area, click on **Add**, and then click on **Configuration Items**.

5.   Under **Available configuration items**, click on **HuDCloud Domain Security Compliance-Account Lock**, and then click on **Add**.

6. Click on **HuDCloud Domain Security Compliance-Password Attributes**, click on **Add**, and then click on **OK**.

7. Click on **Categories**, select **Server**, click on **OK**, and then on **OK** again. Have a look at the following screenshot:

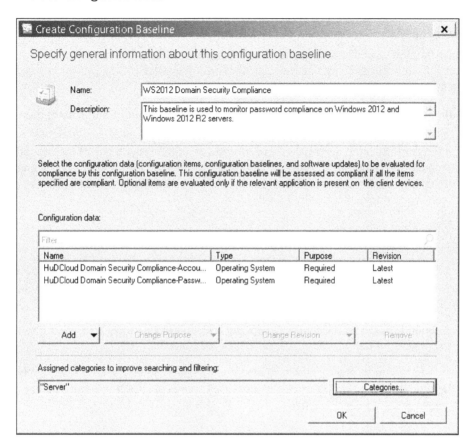

Perform the following steps to deploy this baseline:

1. In the **Configuration Manager Console**, click on **Assets and Compliance**, and then click on the arrow to expand **Compliance Settings**.

2. Click on **Configuration Baselines**, then on the right-hand side, right-click on **WS2012 Domain Security Compliance**, and then click on **Deploy**. The **Deploy Configuration Baselines** page opens.

3. The **WS2012 Domain Security Compliance** configuration baseline is selected by default.

4. In the **Collections** section, click on **Browse**; on the **Select Collection** page, click on the dropdown, and select **Device Collections**; in the **Name** section, click on the collection that contains your test environment servers, for our example, we will click **All Systems**, then click on **OK**, and then click on **OK** again.

How it works...

After importing the `.cab` file, we have all the settings and compliance rules imported into Configuration Manager and can use these to create configuration baselines that evaluate and potentially remediate compliance issues:

1. In the **Configuration Manager Console**, click on **Assets and Compliance**; then, click on the arrow to expand **Compliance Settings**.

2. In the central pane, under **Configuration Items**, right-click on one of the recently imported Configuration Items, and then click on **Properties**. When you click on the **Settings** and **Compliance Rules** tabs, you can see the imported data; you can add, edit, and remove these as required.

There's more...

You can find additional product and operating system baselines; to update the Microsoft Security Compliance Manager, use the following steps that add new operating system and product baselines:

1. Launch the Microsoft Security **Compliance Manager Console**; from the menu at the top, click on **File**, and then click on **Check for Updates**.

2. If there are updates available, click on an update, and then click on **Download**.

3. At the time of writing, a beta for Windows 8.1, Windows 2012 R2, and Internet Explorer (IE) 11 was available.

See also

In order to monitor and remediate group policy settings, you may need to know the registry keys and values associated with those settings. Microsoft provides the Windows registry keys for group policies in a convenient Excel spreadsheet that you can download using the following link:

```
http://www.microsoft.com/en-us/download/details.aspx?id=25250
```

4
Monitoring the Basic Compliance Program

In this chapter, we will cover the following topics:

- ▸ Planning a compliance program for Microsoft System Center 2012 Operations Manager

- ▸ Adding a compliance program monitor in Microsoft System Center 2012 Operations Manager

- ▸ Installing Microsoft System Center 2012 Operations Manager Audit Collection Services to support the compliance program

- ▸ Configuring a compliance program in Microsoft System Center 2012 Operations Manager Audit Collection Services

Introduction

Compliance program regulatory documents, especially data protection laws, define detection, logging, and auditing requirements. An example of such a program is the German Bundesdatenschutzgesetz (BDSG), where you would find the section "to prevent unauthorized usage of data processing systems" in paragraph 9 (`http://www.lw-flyerdruck.de/userfiles/541/File/Dateivorgaben/INFO1_Januar_2011.pdf`). An implication of this requirement could be to detect these unauthorized usages. Microsoft **System Center 2012 Operations Manager** (**SCOM**) has the ability to track and log unauthorized events in Microsoft Active Directory.

Another requirement could be the logging of data access for each individual user. In the **Payment Card Industry Data Security Standard** (**PCI DSS**), requirement 10 states:

> *"10.1 Implement audit trails to link all access to system components to each individual user"*

You can find additional details on PCI DSS at `https://www.pcisecuritystandards.org/documents/PCI_DSS_v3.pdf`.

In this chapter, we will show how to fulfill both requirements with the following SCOM recipes:

- The *Planning a compliance program for Microsoft System Center 2012 Operations Manager* recipe defines the information we need to track and log in the compliance program

- The *Adding a compliance program monitor in Microsoft System Center 2012 Operations Manager* recipe adds a monitor in SCOM to monitor unauthorized logons

- The *Installing Microsoft System Center 2012 Operations Manager Audit Collection Services to support the compliance program* recipe installs the SCOM ACS feature in readiness for logging user access to sensitive data

- The *Configuring a compliance program in Microsoft System Center 2012 Operations Manager Audit Collection Services* recipe defines an SCOM ACS filter to log all data access to a specified folder/network share

The prerequisites for all recipes are as follows:

- You have installed and configured an SCOM infrastructure. You will find detailed information regarding SCOM at `http://technet.microsoft.com/en-us/library/hh205987.aspx`.

- You have installed and configured Microsoft SQL Server.

> It is recommended that you use a separate SCOM management server for the **Audit Collection Services** (**ACS**) feature. This is due to the higher workload the ACS needs.
>
> Additionally, it is recommended that you use a dedicated SQL Server or SQL Server Instance for the ACS database. The reason is that a more restrictive access policy to the data in this database will prevent manual manipulation of the data.

- The monitor and the ACS in SCOM will read the event log of the monitored servers, such as Active Directory domain controllers and, in the example used in this recipe, a file server. To log these events in the local security event log on the server, you have to activate logging on each server locally or centralized with a Group Policy.

    1. To activate the auditing, open a GPO in the **Group Policy Management Editor**.

2. Navigate to **Computer Configuration | Policies | Windows Settings | Security Settings | Local Policies | Audit Policy**.

3. Open the **Audit object access** policy and check the **Define these policy settings**, **Success**, and **Failure** options as shown in the following screenshot:

4. Open **Audit logon events** and check the **Define these policy settings** and **Failure** options as follows:

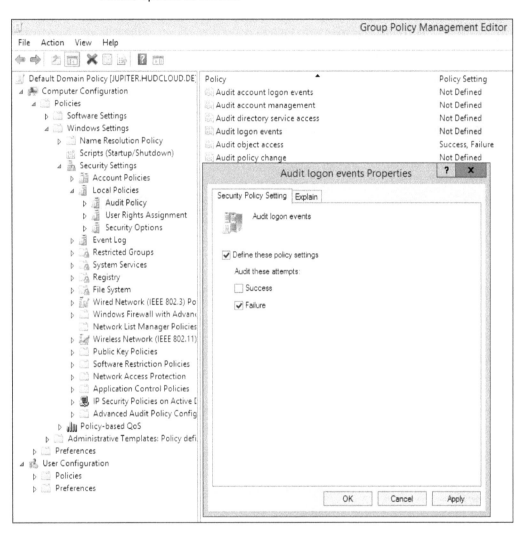

Planning a compliance program for Microsoft System Center 2012 Operations Manager

To log all the required information and events in SCOM, we need to plan the compliance program. The planning includes identifying the data we need to audit and the events in Active Directory.

Getting ready

Before starting with detailed planning, you need to study the compliance regulatory documents (internal and external) to get the details of the information you need to log and audit.

In the recipes of this chapter, we will focus on the following two different scenarios:

▶ Monitoring Active Directory for failed logons caused by a brute-force attack

 You can find more details on brute-force attacks at `http://en.wikipedia.org/wiki/Brute-force_attack`.

▶ Monitoring and logging any access to files in a shared folder on a server

How to do it...

The following sections will show you how to plan the needed details.

Monitoring failed logons caused by a brute-force attack

The planning details to fulfill the requirements of this compliance program are mentioned in the following table:

Monitored system	Events to monitor	Criteria of monitor
All domain controllers	All failed logons in Active Directory	Amount of failed logons within a specified time. In our recipe, we will use *10 failed logon attempts in 60 seconds*. Event ID: `4625`

Logging any access to files in a shared folder on a server

The planning details to fulfill the compliance program requirements are mentioned in the following table:

Monitored system	Events to monitor	Criteria of monitor
File server named Jupiter	All access (failed and succeeded) to all files in a specified folder.	▸ Name of the folder to monitor on server: `Data` ▸ Event ID: `4663` and `4646`

How it works...

In the planning phase, use the questions given in the coming sections to gather the required details.

Monitoring failed logons caused by a brute-force attack

▸ Which servers or systems need to be monitored?

  ❑ To monitor failed logon events caused by a brute-force attack, we will focus on monitoring all domain controllers in Active Directory

▸ Which events need to be logged?

  ❑ To monitor failed logon events caused by a brute-force attack, we will focus on the failed logon events only—Event ID `4625` in the security event log of all domain controllers

▸ Which specific details need to be monitored?

  ❑ We defined the critical amount of failed logon events within an interval—10 failed logon attempts within 60 seconds

Logging any access to files in a shared folder on a server

▸ Which servers or systems need to be monitored?

  ❑ We will monitor the Jupiter file server

▸ Which events need to be logged?

  ❑ To monitor all data access events, failed and successful, on all data in the `Data` folder

▸ Which specific details does the monitor need?

  ❑ Event IDs for data access are `4663` and `4656`

There's more...

What we discussed in this recipe is just one example showing how to plan the monitoring of compliance-program-related issues.

Defining other compliance program events to monitor

Besides the two scenarios in this chapter, you can monitor different events on your servers and IT systems.

A list of Windows Security Log Event IDs can be found at `http://www.ultimatewindowssecurity.com/securitylog/encyclopedia/Default.aspx`.

Adding a compliance program monitor in Microsoft System Center 2012 Operations Manager

In accordance with a compliance regulatory document, such as PCI DSS, it is required to monitor failed logon attempts that can be caused by a brute-force attack. In a brute-force attack, a script or program is used to guess a password by automatically trying different combinations of characters.

This recipe describes how to monitor and log this kind of compliance issue with Microsoft System Center 2012 Operations Manager.

Getting ready

To create a monitor in SCOM 2012, an installed and configured SCOM 2012 server is required. You must also review the *Planning a compliance program for Microsoft System Center 2012 Operations Manager* recipe in this chapter.

The configuration of the monitor in SCOM 2012 is stored in a management pack. Perform the following steps to create a new management pack for this recipe:

1. Open the SCOM 2012 console.
2. Navigate to **Administration | Management Packs**.
3. Click on the **Create Management Pack** task in the **Tasks** pane.
4. Enter a name in the **Name:** field. In our recipe, we will use **Compliance program failed logon events**.
5. In the **Description:** field, enter the following text: `This Management Pack contains the configuration to monitor failed logon events`.
6. Click on **Next**.
7. Click on **Create**.

How to do it...

Open the Operations Manager console and perform the steps given in the coming sections to create a new monitor to log failed logon attempts.

Creating a group in SCOM 2012

Groups in SCOM 2012 are helpful in combining related items that should be monitored or configured in the same way. Perform the following steps to create a group:

1. Open the SCOM 2012 console.

2. Navigate to the **Authoring in SCOM 2012** console.

3. In the left-hand side pane, mark **Groups** and click on **Create a New Group** in the **Tasks** pane.

4. Enter AD Domain Controllers (Compliance Program) in the **Name:** field.

5. Enter Contains all AD domain controllers for audit in a compliance program in the **Description:** field.

6. Select the management pack **Compliance program failed logon events** we created earlier in the *Getting ready* section.

   The preceding steps are shown in the following screenshot:

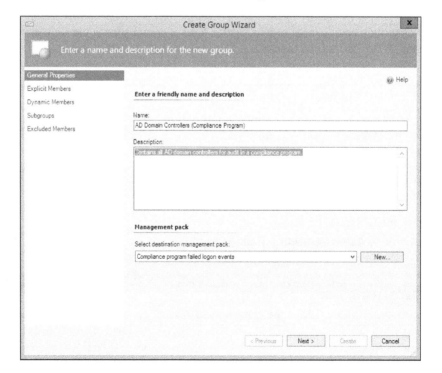

7. Click on **Next**.

8. In the **Explicit Members** section, add the domain controllers by clicking on the **Add/Remove Objects** button.

9. In the **Search for:** field, select **Windows Server**.

10. Add the computer name of the DC in the **Filter by part of name (optional):** field. In our environment, the name of the domain controller is Jupiter and DC2.

11. Mark the computer in the **Available items** list, and click on **Add**.

12. Repeat steps 10 and 11 for all your domain controllers. The following screenshot illustrates the mentioned steps:

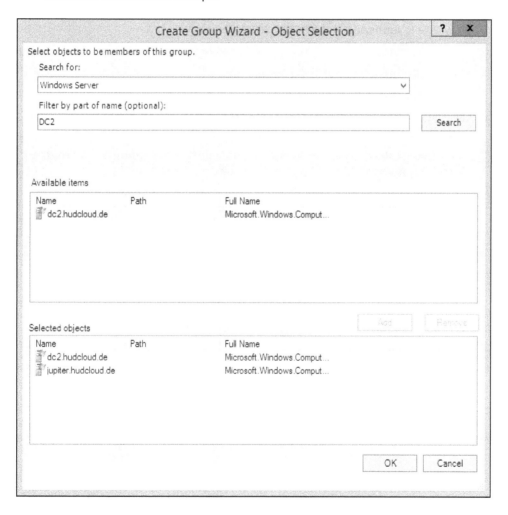

13. Click on **OK**.

14. Click on **Next**

15. In the **Dynamic Members** section, click on **Next**.

16. In the **Subgroups** section, click on **Next**.

17. In the **Excluded Members** section, click on **Create**.

Creating a monitor in SCOM 2012

Perform the following steps to create a monitor:

1. Open the SCOM 2012 console.

2. Navigate to **Authoring** in the SCOM 2012 console.

3. In the left-hand side pane, expand **Management Pack Objects** and click on **Monitor**.

4. Click on **Create a Monitor** in the **Tasks** pane.

5. Select **Unit Monitor**.

6. Navigate to **Windows Events | Repeated Event Detection | Timer Reset** on the **Create a unit monitor** page.

7. In the **Select destination management pack:** field, select **Compliance program failed logon events**. Have a look at the following screenshot:

8. Click on **Next**.

9. On the **General** tab, add `Failed logon attempts (more than x failed logons within y minutes)` in the **Name:** field.

10. In the **Description (optional):** field, add `Compliance program alert threshold of failed attempts reached.`

11. Next to the **Monitor target** field, click on **Select …**, select **Windows Server**, and click on **OK**.

12. In the **Parent monitor:** field, select **Security**. Have a look at the following screenshot:

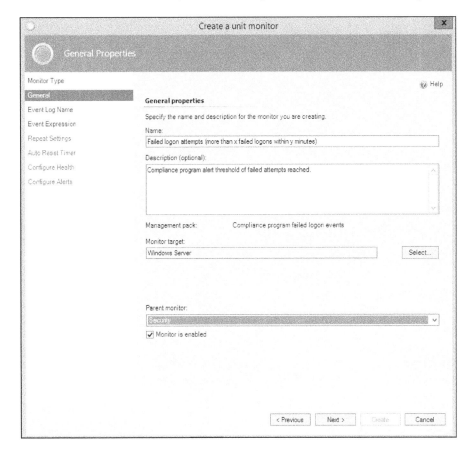

13. Uncheck **Monitor is enabled**.

14. Click on **Next**.

15. On the **Event Log Name** page, select **Security** for the **Log Name** field.

16. Click on **Next**.

17. In the **Event Expression** page, enter `4625` in the **Event ID Value** field.

18. In the **Event Source** row, select **Operator Contains**.

19. Add `Microsoft Windows security auditing` in the **Value** field. Have a look at the following screenshot:

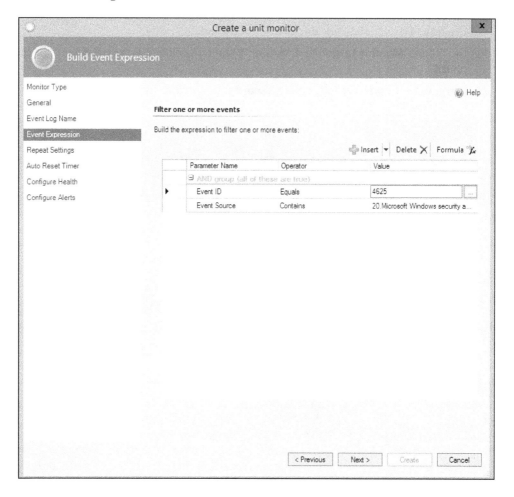

20. Click on **Next**.

21. In the **Repeat Settings** page, select **Trigger on count, sliding** in the **Counting Mode:** field.

22. Select **10** in the **Compare Count:** field. Have a look at the following screenshot:

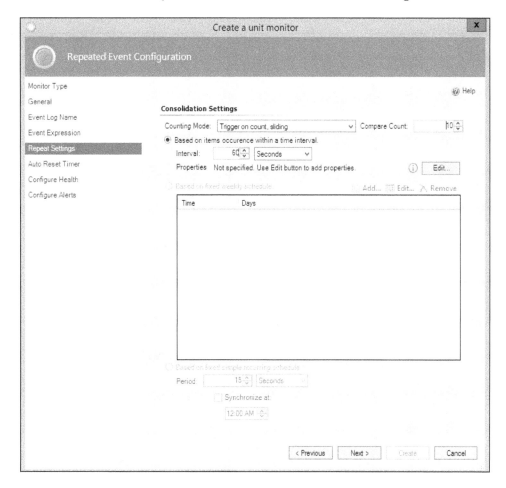

23. Click on **Next**.

24. In the **Auto Reset Timer** page, select **60 Seconds**.

25. Click on **Next**.

> Depending on your company policy of firewall configuration, it might be required to add a firewall rule for **Agent (Audit Collection Services (ACS) forwarder)** on port 51909 (`http://technet.microsoft.com/en-us/library/jj656649.aspx`).

26. In the **Configure Health** page, select **Critical** for the **Repeated Event Raised** entry. Have a look at the following screenshot:

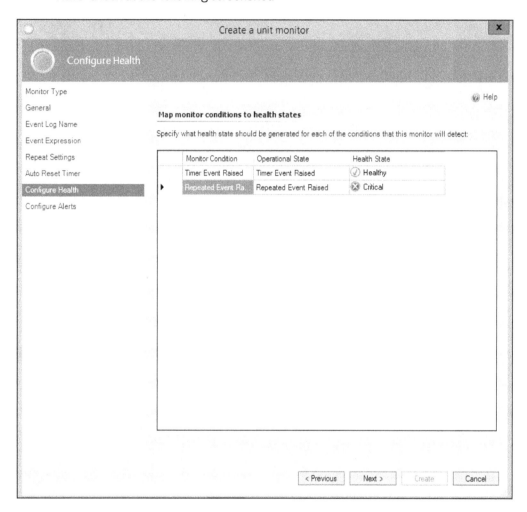

27. Click on **Next**.

28. On the **Configure Alerts** page, select the **Generate alerts for this monitor** checkbox and click on **Create**.

29. Select the monitor created in the list in the central pane of the SCOM 2012 console and right-click on it.

30. Navigate to **Override the Monitor | For a group**.

31. Add **AD Domain Controllers (Compliance Program)**.

32. Mark the checkbox in the row **Enabled**, and select **True** in the **Override Value** column. Have a look at the following screenshot:

33. Click on **OK**.

How it works...

The monitor you created will raise and log an event when the following conditions are met:

▸ Failed logons on any Domain Controller in the Active Directory 10 times in a row within 60 seconds.

▸ The monitor is only active on domain controllers filtered by a manually created group.

▸ A critical status will be shown in the SCOM console for the domain controller. The Active Directory is a shared service; this means the logon request might be shared between different domain controllers.

There's more...

After the monitor is configured in SCOM, the monitor needs to be tested.

Testing the created compliance program monitor

To test the monitor you created in SCOM, run the following script in a command prompt on any computer within the Active Directory domain:

```
set /a x=1
:Start
net use o: \\<Name of a monitored Domain Controller\c$ /
User:Administrator hjghkgkjhgkjg
set /a x=%x%+1
if %x% NEQ 20 goto Start
```

Wait for a few minutes to let SCOM 2012 process the monitoring, and then perform the following steps:

1. Open the SCOM console.

2. Navigate to **Monitoring | Compliance program failed logon events | Max failed logon attempts alerts**.

You will see an alert in the list that is related to the monitor we created, as shown in the following screenshot:

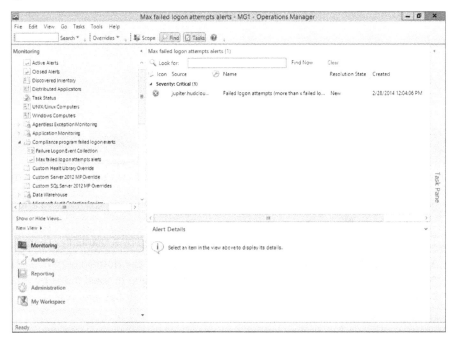

See also

The following official web links are a great source of the most up-to-date information:

- ▶ **Microsoft TechNet Library**: The *Tuning Monitoring by Using Targeting and Overrides* article at `http://technet.microsoft.com/en-us/library/hh230704.aspx`

- ▶ **Microsoft TechNet Library**: The *Monitors and Rules* article at `http://technet.microsoft.com/en-us/library/hh457603.aspx`

- ▶ **System Center Central**: The *Windows 2008 Active Directory Security Audit MP (for SCE 2010 and OpsMgr 2007 R2)* article `http://www.systemcentercentral.com/pack-catalog/windows-2008-active-directory-security-audit-mp-for-sce-2010-and-opsmgr-2007-r2/`

Installing Microsoft System Center 2012 Operations Manager Audit Collection Services to support the compliance program

This recipe describe the steps to install and configure the **Microsoft System Center 2012 Operations Manager Audit Collection Services** (**SCOM ACS**).

Getting ready

To install the SCOM ACS, you need an installed and configured SCOM 2012 server. Also, you need access to a Microsoft SQL Server default instance or named instance to deploy the ACS database. A Microsoft SQL Server Reporting Service instance is required before starting this recipe.

 It is a recommended practice to use a separated Microsoft SQL Server instance for the ACS database.

How to do it...

The following steps will let you set up the Microsoft System Center 2012 Operations Manager Audit Collection Services:

1. Insert the SCOM installation media.
2. Start **Setup.exe**.

3. Click on **Audit collection services**. Have a look at the following screenshot:

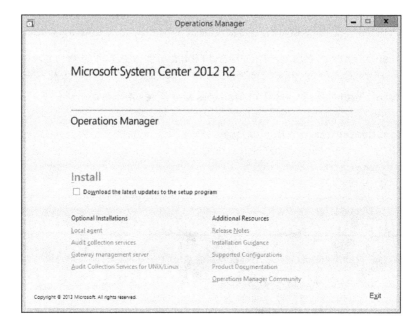

4. Click on **Next**.
5. Select **I accept the license terms**.
6. Click on **Next**.
7. Check **Create a new database**. Have a look at the following screenshot:

8. Click on **Next**.

9. On the **Data Source** window, keep the default name of **Data source name** and click on **Next**.

10. Select **Remote database server**.

11. Provide the name of the Microsoft SQL Server in the **Remote database server machine name** field. Optionally, you can add the name of the SQL instance name:

12. Click on **Next**.

13. Select **Windows authentication**.

14. Click on **Next**.

15. Select **SQL Server's default data and log file directories** (or use a different location if needed).

16. Click on **Next**.

17. Type `180` in the **Number of days an event is retained in database:** field. Have a look at the following screenshot:

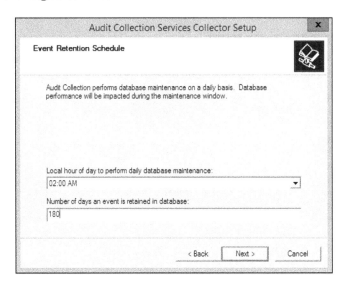

18. Click on **Next**.

19. Select **Local** in the **Choose the timestamp format:** section or select **Universal Coordinated Time (UTC)** if your enterprise and SCOM environment is spread over different time zones.

20. Click on **Next**.

21. On the **Summary** page, click on **Next**.

22. Click on **OK** and provide the credentials for the Microsoft SQL Server login if requested. Have a look at the following screenshot:

23. Click on **Finish**.

The next set of steps will let you set up Audit Report Deployment:

1. Create a folder on the server where ACS is installed named C:\ACS.

2. Copy the folder content of the SCOM 2012 installation media <cddrive>:\\ ReportModels\acs to C:\ACS. Have a look at the following screenshot:

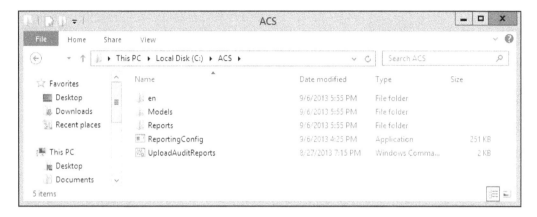

3. Open the command prompt with the option **Run as administrator**.

4. Change the directory in the command prompt to C:\ACS.

5. Run the following command in the command prompt (in one line, and replace the values between < and > with the related values):

```
UploadAuditReports <SQL Server\Instance> <URL of SQL Reporting
Server > <Path of the copied ACS folder>
```

```
UploadAuditReports "SCOM2012R2ACS" "http://SCOM2012R2ACS/
ReportServer" "C:\ACS"
```

The following screenshot shows an example:

```
C:\ACS>UploadAuditReports SCOM2012R2ACS http://SCOM2012R2ACS/ReportServer C:\ACS
Warning(s) Loading file C:\ACS\Models\Audit.smdl:

Warning(s) Loading file C:\ACS\Models\Audit5.smdl:


C:\ACS>_
```

The warnings can be ignored. Depending on the configuration of your SQL Reporting Service, it might be required to use https instead of http to deploy the Audit Reports.

How it works...

Microsoft System Center 2012 Operations Manager Audit Collection Services will be installed, and the SCOM 2012 ACS Reports are deployed to the specified Microsoft SQL Server Reporting Service.

There's more...

After the ACS reports are deployed, the results can be checked on the SQL Reporting Server.

Checking whether ACS reports are installed

To check whether the ACS reports are installed, perform the following steps:

1. Open Internet Explorer on the SCOM 2012 ACS server.

2. Navigate to the URL of the Reporting Server. In our example, it is `http://SCOM2012R2ACS/ReportServer`.

3. Open the `Audit Reports` folder.

4. The list of reports should look like the following screenshot:

scom2012r2acs/ReportServer - /Audit Reports

```
[To Parent Directory]
    Friday, February 14, 2014 7:04 AM      17814 Access Violation - Account Locked
    Friday, February 14, 2014 7:05 AM     100991 Access Violation - Unsuccessful Logon Attempts
    Friday, February 14, 2014 7:05 AM      39504 Account Management - Domain and Built-in Administrators Changes
    Friday, February 14, 2014 7:05 AM      26029 Account Management - Passwords Change Attempts by Non-owner
    Friday, February 14, 2014 7:05 AM      40976 Account Management - User Accounts Created
    Friday, February 14, 2014 7:05 AM      40966 Account Management - User Accounts Deleted
    Friday, February 14, 2014 7:04 AM      67896 Audit
    Friday, February 14, 2014 7:05 AM      38183 Audit Report Template
    Friday, February 14, 2014 7:04 AM      44405 Audit5
    Friday, February 14, 2014 7:05 AM      50243 Audit5 Report Template
    Friday, February 14, 2014 7:05 AM      64719 DAC - Central Access Policy For File Changes
    Friday, February 14, 2014 7:05 AM      60703 DAC - File Resource Property Changes
    Friday, February 14, 2014 7:05 AM      62254 DAC - Object Access 1 Resource Attribute Query
    Friday, February 14, 2014 7:05 AM      63116 DAC - Object Access 2 Resource Attribute Query
    Friday, February 14, 2014 7:05 AM      64385 DAC - Object Access 3 Resource Attribute Query
    Friday, February 14, 2014 7:05 AM      57130 DAC - Object Attribute Changes
    Friday, February 14, 2014 7:05 AM      51817 DAC - Staging
    Friday, February 14, 2014 7:04 AM      <ds> DB Audit
    Friday, February 14, 2014 7:05 AM      52499 Forensic - All Events For Specified Computer
    Friday, February 14, 2014 7:05 AM      55152 Forensic - All Events For Specified User
    Friday, February 14, 2014 7:05 AM      51696 Forensic - All Events With Specified Event ID
    Friday, February 14, 2014 7:05 AM      47921 Planning - Event Counts
    Friday, February 14, 2014 7:05 AM      47519 Planning - Event Counts by Computer
    Friday, February 14, 2014 7:05 AM      22779 Planning - Hourly Event Distribution
    Friday, February 14, 2014 7:05 AM      68114 Planning - Logon Counts of Privileged Users
    Friday, February 14, 2014 7:05 AM      18443 Policy - Account Policy Changed
    Friday, February 14, 2014 7:05 AM      21269 Policy - Audit Policy Changed
    Friday, February 14, 2014 7:05 AM      29153 Policy - Object Permissions Changed
    Friday, February 14, 2014 7:05 AM      23229 Policy - Privilege Added Or Removed
    Friday, February 14, 2014 7:05 AM      29619 System Integrity - Audit Failure
    Friday, February 14, 2014 7:05 AM      38099 System Integrity - Audit Log Cleared
    Friday, February 14, 2014 7:05 AM      41083 Usage - Object Access
    Friday, February 14, 2014 7:05 AM      44352 Usage - Privileged logon
    Friday, February 14, 2014 7:05 AM      38403 Usage - Sensitive Security Groups Changes
    Friday, February 14, 2014 7:05 AM     103122 Usage - User Logon

Microsoft SQL Server Reporting Services Version 11.0.2100.60
```

See also

▶ The *Audit Collection Services (ACS)* article in the Microsoft TechNet library at
`http://technet.microsoft.com/en-us/library/bb381258.aspx`

Configuring a compliance program in Microsoft System Center 2012 Operations Manager Audit Collection Services

After the installation of ACS, the ACS forwarders send all events to the ACS collector. The ACS collector processes the data and sends the data to the ACS database.

We have to filter to ensure only specified events are stored in the database. These events are of Event IDs `4663` and `4656`.

In this recipe, we will configure the Microsoft System Center 2012 Operations Manager Audit Collection Services to log the events we planned in the *Planning a compliance program for Microsoft System Center 2012 Operations Manager* recipe.

Two steps are need for this:

▶ Configuring the Microsoft System Center 2012 Operations Manager Audit Collection Services Collector

▶ Configuring the Microsoft System Center 2012 Operations Manager Audit Collection Services Forwarder

Getting ready

To configure the SCOM ACS Collector and the SCOM ACS Forwarder, the following preparation needs to be done:

▶ Set up a healthy and operational Active Directory.

▶ Install a healthy and operational Microsoft System Center 2012 Operations Manager Server

▶ Finish the planning phase of the compliance program

▶ Install Microsoft System Center 2012 Operations Manager Audit Collection Services

Setting permissions in the registry key on the SCOM 2012 ACS Server

The permissions on a registry key needs to be modified on the server running the SCOM 2012 ACS. This is due to incorrect permissions being set during the setup. Perform the following steps:

1. Open `Regedit.exe` on the server running the SCOM 2012 ACS.

2. Navigate to `HKEY_LOCAL_MACHINE\SYSTEM\CurrentControlSet\Services\AdtServer\Parameters`.

3. Right-click on **Parameters** and select **Permissions**. Have a look at the following screenshot:

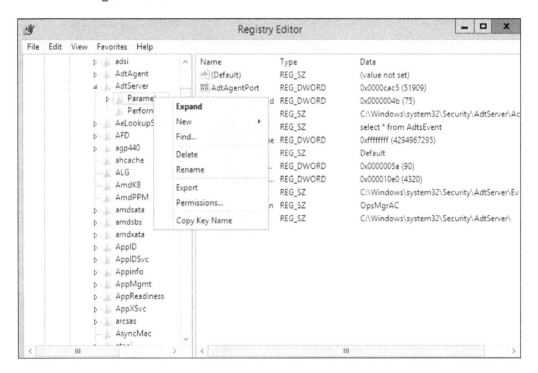

4. Click on **Advanced**.

5. Select **NETWORK SERVICE** from the list and click on **Edit**.

6. Click on **Show advanced permissions**.

7. Select **Applies to: This key and subkeys**.

8. Select the following under **Advanced permissions**, and have a look at the screenshot that comes after the following list of advanced permissions:

    ❑   **Query Value**

    ❑   **Set Value**

    ❑   **Enumerate Subkeys**

    ❑   **Notify**

    ❑   **Read Control**

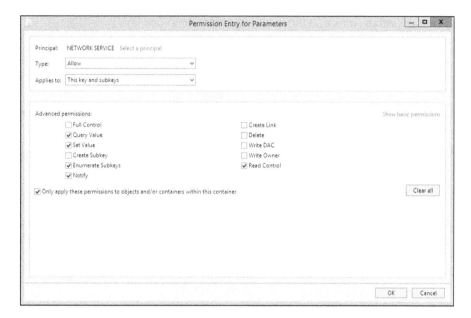

9. Click on **OK** in the **Permission Entry for Parameters** window.
10. Click on **OK** in the **Advanced Security Settings for Parameters** window.
11. Click on **OK** in the **Permissions for Parameter** window.
12. Close the **Registry Editor**.

Copying the required files from the SCOM 2012 installation media

Copy the following files from the SCOM 2012 installation media to the local folder
`C:\ACS` that we already created in the recipe before on the SCOM 2012 ACS server:

▶   `<Installationmedia:>\acs\AMD64\ADTAdmin.exe`

▶   `<Installationmedia:>\acs\AMD64\OmacAdmn.dll`

The `ADTAdmin.exe` is used in the *How to do it...* section.

How to do it...

To configure the compliance program in SCOM 2012 ACS perform the steps given in the following sections.

Creating an ACS Filter on the SCOM 2012 ACS server

1. Open the command prompt with the option **Run as administrator**.

2. Change the directory to C:\ACS.

3. Run ADTAmdin.exe with the following parameters (one line!):

```
AdtAdmin.exe -setquery -Collector:SCOM2012R2ACS -query:"Select
* from AdtsEvent WHERE ((EventID=4663 or EventID=4656) and not
PrimaryUser like '%$')"
```

Activating the Microsoft System Center 2012 Operations Manager Audit Collection Services Forwarder

Perform the following steps:

1. Open the SCOM console on the SCOM ACS server.

2. Navigate to **Monitoring | Operations Manager | Agent Health State**.

3. Select the server in the **Agent State** section, which should forward security events to the ACS Audit Collector. In this recipe, the server name is Jupiter and is the server we wish to monitor for the identified events in the security event log.

4. Click on **Enable Audit Collection** in the **Tasks** pane. Have a look at the following screenshot:

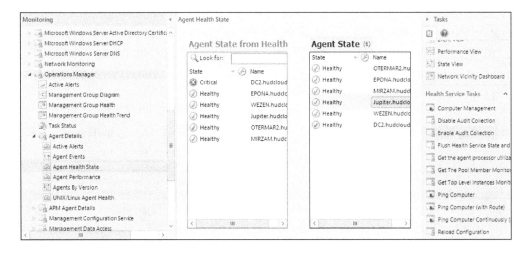

5. Click on **Override** in the newly opened **RunTask – Enable Audit Collection** window as shown in the following screenshot:

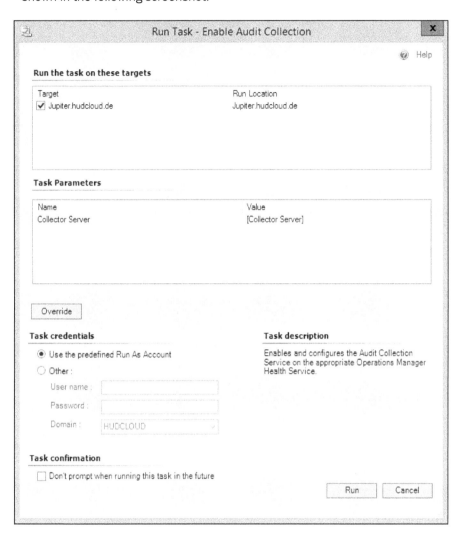

6. Enter the ACS Collector server in the **New Value** field in the **Override Task Parameters** form. In our environment, the server name is **SCOM2012R2ACS**. Have a look at the following screenshot:

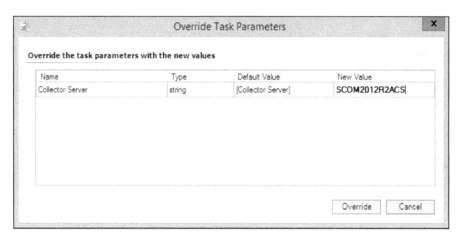

7. Click on **Override**.
8. Click on **Run** in the **Run Task – Enable Audit Collection** window.
9. Click on **Close**. Have a look at the following screenshot:

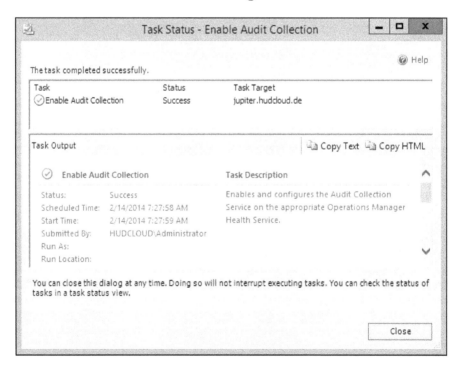

Activating auditing on a folder of the file server

1. Open **File Explorer** on the file server.

2. Navigate to the drive and folder we need to audit. In our example, it is the folder C:\Data.

3. Right-click on the folder and select **Properties**.

4. Click on the **Security** tab.

5. Click on **Advanced**.

6. Click on the **Auditing** tab. Have a look at the following screenshot:

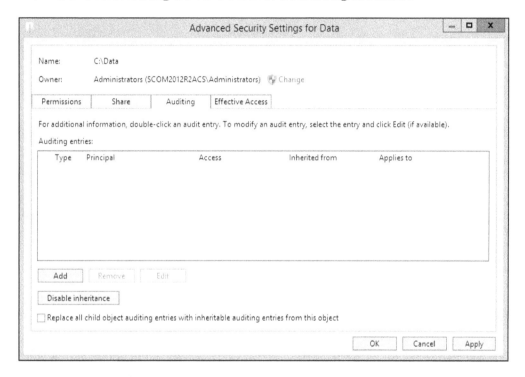

7. Click on **Add**.

8. Click on **Select a principal** and add **Everyone** to the list.

9. Select **All** in the **Type** field.

10. Check that **This folder, subfolders and files** is selected in the **Applies to** field.

11. Select **Full control** in the **Basic permissions** section. Have a look at the following screenshot:

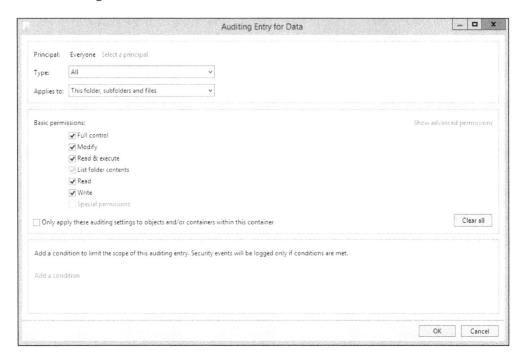

12. Click on **OK** in the **Auditing Entry for Data** window.

13. Click on **OK** in the **Advanced Security Settings for Data** window.

14. Click on **OK** in the **Data Properties** window.

How it works...

In the first step of this recipe, a filter is defined that logs the event in the SCOM 2012 ACS database on the SCOM 2012 ACS server. To log all file and folder events, we are using the Event IDs 4663 and 4656 as defined in the compliance program planning. Using a filter prevents the logging of unnecessary information in the SCOM 2012 ACS database.

In the next step, the SCOM 2012 ACS Forwarder on the monitored file server will be activated and configured; the server name of the file server is Jupiter in our example. The SCOM 2012 Forwarder will send the audit data to the SCOM 2012 ACS collector server.

In the last step, the required audit events are defined on the file server (in our example, the server name is Jupiter). As stated in our planned and defined compliance program, we need to audit all file and folder accesses for all users.

There's more...

It is possible to check the ACS Forwarder configuration and filter after the initial configuration is done.

Check the ACS Forwarder configuration on the audited server

To check the settings of the ACS Forwarder on the audited server, perform the following steps:

1. Open the Services console (`Services.msc`) on the audited server. In our example, the server name is `Jupiter`.

2. Check the settings and state of the **Microsoft Monitoring Agent Audit Forwarding** service.

The **Status** of the service should be **Running**, and the **Startup Type** should be **Automatic**.

Checking the auditing filter on the SCOM 2012 ACS server

The following steps describe how to check the SCOM 2012 ACS collector filter we configured earlier in this chapter:

1. Open the command prompt with the option **Run as administrator** on the SCOM 2012 ACS server.

2. Change the directory to `C:\ACS`.

3. Run the following command (one line):

   `AdtAdmin.exe /getquery /Collector:<Servername of the SCOM2012 ACS server>`

   The following screenshot shows the output:

```
C:\ACS>AdtAdmin.exe /getquery /Collector:SCOM2012R2ACS
Current query: 'Select * from AdtsEvent WHERE ((EventID=4663 or EventID=4656) and not (PrimaryUser like 'z$')>'
C:\ACS>_
```

Checking the audit data for the specified folder in the SCOM 2012 ACS database

To check the audit data in the SCOM 2012 ACS database, perform the following steps:

1. Open the SQL Server Management Studio console on the Microsoft SQL Server where the ACS database is configured.

2. Open a new query window and run the following SQL query:

```
Use OperationsManagerAC
SELECT TOP 1000 [Id]
        , [EventId]
        , [SequenceNo]
        , [S/F]
        , [Category]
        , [CreationTime]
        , [CollectionTime]
        , [AgentMachine]
        , [EventMachine]
        , [Source]
        , [HeaderSid]
        , [HeaderUser]
        , [HeaderDomain]
        , [PrimarySid]
        , [PrimaryUser]
        , [PrimaryDomain]
        , [PrimaryLogonId]
        , [ClientSid]
        , [ClientUser]
        , [ClientDomain]
        , [ClientLogonId]
        , [TargetSid]
        , [TargetUser]
        , [TargetDomain]
        , [String01]
        , [String02]
        , [String03]
```

```
, [String04]

, [String05]

, [String06]

, [String07]

, [String08]

, [String09]

, [String10]

, [String11]

, [String12]

, [String13]

, [String14]

, [String15]

, [String16]

, [String17]

, [String18]

, [String19]

, [String20]

, [String21]

, [String22]

    FROM [OperationsManagerAC].[AdtServer].[dvAll] where (EventId =
4656 or EventId = 4663) and PrimaryUser not like '%$' and String02
like'%C:\Data%'

Order By CreationTime DESC
```

The result should look like the following screenshot:

	Id	EventId	SequenceNo	S/F	Category	CreationTime	CollectionTime	AgentMachine	EventMachine
1	80	4656	-452972296	S	OBJECTACCESS_FILESYSTEM	2014-02-28 13:26:34.000	2014-02-28 13:26:34.980	HUDCLOUD\JUPITER$	Jupiter.hudcloud.de
2	81	4656	-452972292	S	OBJECTACCESS_FILESYSTEM	2014-02-28 13:26:34.000	2014-02-28 13:26:34.980	HUDCLOUD\JUPITER$	Jupiter.hudcloud.de
3	82	4663	-452972291	S	OBJECTACCESS_FILESYSTEM	2014-02-28 13:26:34.000	2014-02-28 13:26:34.980	HUDCLOUD\JUPITER$	Jupiter.hudcloud.de
4	83	4656	-452972286	S	OBJECTACCESS_FILESYSTEM	2014-02-28 13:26:34.000	2014-02-28 13:26:34.980	HUDCLOUD\JUPITER$	Jupiter.hudcloud.de
5	84	4663	-452972285	S	OBJECTACCESS_FILESYSTEM	2014-02-28 13:26:34.000	2014-02-28 13:26:34.980	HUDCLOUD\JUPITER$	Jupiter.hudcloud.de
6	85	4656	-452972255	S	OBJECTACCESS_FILESYSTEM	2014-02-28 13:26:34.000	2014-02-28 13:26:34.980	HUDCLOUD\JUPITER$	Jupiter.hudcloud.de
7	86	4663	-452972254	S	OBJECTACCESS_FILESYSTEM	2014-02-28 13:26:34.000	2014-02-28 13:26:34.980	HUDCLOUD\JUPITER$	Jupiter.hudcloud.de
8	87	4656	-452972141	S	OBJECTACCESS_FILESYSTEM	2014-02-28 13:26:34.000	2014-02-28 13:26:34.980	HUDCLOUD\JUPITER$	Jupiter.hudcloud.de
9	88	4663	-452972140	S	OBJECTACCESS_FILESYSTEM	2014-02-28 13:26:34.000	2014-02-28 13:26:34.980	HUDCLOUD\JUPITER$	Jupiter.hudcloud.de
10	89	4656	-452972135	S	OBJECTACCESS_FILESYSTEM	2014-02-28 13:26:34.000	2014-02-28 13:26:35.120	HUDCLOUD\JUPITER$	Jupiter.hudcloud.de

How to get a report of the SCOM 2012 ACS data will be described in *Chapter 9, Reporting on Compliance with System Center 2012.*

See also

- The *Collecting Security Events Using Audit Collection Services in Operations Manager* article of Microsoft TechNet Library at `http://technet.microsoft.com/en-us/library/hh212908.aspx`

5
Starting an Enterprise Compliance Program

In this chapter, we will cover the following topics:

- ▸ Using project management in your compliance approach
- ▸ Understanding management support
- ▸ Defining your communication approach
- ▸ Planning the risk assessment approach
- ▸ Planning documentation requirements
- ▸ Defining your test approach

Introduction

The belief that a company will never face a security or compliance incident is rather naive but still held by many business managers. They would rather maintain their reactive approach than invest time and money in a proactive, systematic approach. Should an issue arise or a business unit receive a high degree of public attention, the incident is addressed, and this process of doing so has come to be known as a **compliance program**.

To exaggerate this a little, imagine the following series of events:

1. Find out that you have an issue
2. Start panicking
3. Get management buy-in to throw money and time at the issue

4. Implement your solution as publicly as possible to show what a great job you are doing

5. Pray that the issue is truly addressed

In other words, what is happening here is that the issue is identified and addressed, but there is never a true assessment of the general environment or the value of the issue addressed.

Based on my experience, this reactive approach wastes time and money. Policies, processes, and controls are written or rewritten to reflect the new issue. Generally, reactive training reaches all or just the affected employees. However, as soon as the redesigning of policies, controls, and training is complete, everyone falls back into the accustomed way of doing business. New employees don't necessarily receive training and thus are not aware that certain policies and/or processes should be followed and why they have been introduced. Malpractices that might have led to the issue are never truly addressed as the company culture stays as before.

A more proactive approach to a compliance program will allow you to understand the following:

▸ Where your sensitive information is processed and how it flows through the company to identify potentially overlooked areas

▸ The preceding point will lead to a question, "What other areas should be addressed if sensitive information is residing on noncompliant systems?"

▸ What percentage of employees understands its responsibilities and knows how to recognize and report incidents

The preceding statements are just three questions, but there are many more that can be addressed for a meaningful compliance program that will help generate benefits for the business.

To summarize, if your company wants to implement a compliance program and you are supposed to lead it, do not start with a reactive compliance program. If you do this, it is just like a leak in the roof of a house. Putting a bucket under the leak will stop the water from filling up inside the house, but the core issue is not yet addressed and you do not know if there is a larger problem lurking around. With a systematic approach, you will be able to look at the whole roof, and not just the first leak, to get an understanding of what you are facing. Based on these findings, prioritize your next steps and spend money where it will be most effective.

The recipes provided in this chapter will inform you about the six most important aspects to succeed with your compliance program.

Using project management in your compliance approach

Using project management for a systematic approach to establish a compliance program is the first important aspect to be considered for a successful implementation. Many companies already have processes for project management; defined documents to use for the initiation or proposal of a project; and documents for project plans, budgets, resources, and time plans. In addition to the processes, they also have documents on how to deal with reviews on overspending, delays, and so on. If not, there are many great books on project management that will help you with these issues. This book will not go into more details on project management. Instead, it will focus on the aspects that are most important for a successful compliance project.

Getting ready

Understanding project management is an important area of a compliance program. Where necessary, you should consider attending training, buying a book, or working with an internal project manager. This will ensure the compliance program is achievable in a timely manner and runs smoothly throughout its duration.

How to do it...

Focusing on the compliance aspect of your project, the steps discussed in the following sections must be worked through.

Step 1 – defining and understanding the reason for your company's compliance program

Essentially, you have to answer the following question: *"Why is the compliance program important to your business?"*

To answer this question, the first thing you must understand is that compliance is not only an IT project, but also a business one. This means you have to translate the compliance risks that are centered on IT, and can be solved with IT solutions, into business terms.

In addition, always keep in mind that every employee should be able to understand what compliance and risk, addressed by the compliance project, mean. You have to tell them why it is important for their work.

The answer will vary, and it is subject to the employee's role within the business. For example, a help desk employee will have a different perspective on the company and its operations when compared to that of a business unit line manager.

The next paragraphs provide an example on how and why most business managers do not care about data protection laws. Data protection is rarely a conversational topic they will get excited about. Therefore, it might never seem important enough for their agenda: for them, this is likely to be something that belongs to the IT agenda. To ensure business managers appreciate and understand the necessity and value of a compliance project, you may have to translate the topic into their business language. There are numerous ways to do this:

▶ Identify security breaches or other incidents where compliance requirements have been breached within your own company. The consequences of these incidents would have had a negative impact on your business. Research how your compliance program should have prevented this incident. This is, after all, why you are undertaking the project. Do not just look at incidents, but talk to the sales and legal departments as well. There might be instances of missed sales or opportunities because the company wasn't able to prove its compliance or adherence to IT security standards.

▶ Research on the Internet and in magazines. Also, talk to lawyers or external sources to know about the companies in your industry (!) that failed to adequately protect individual data that led to the publication of their name in the news and landed the directors in court with losses to their reputation or revenues. These incidents must be real and not older than 12 months.

▶ Research on areas with a high likelihood of occurrences, such as malware or hacking incidents, and provide statistical information showing that, just because you have not been hit yet, the probability of a future occurrence is high. There are numerous studies available. Presenting this statistical information has more of an impact than just talking about antivirus infections leading to loss of data.

▶ Research on topics that currently have high public attention, for example, espionage, spyware, or terrorism. These are topics that may already be in the minds of people in the business. Therefore, they may be able to connect with the staff easily using these as a reference.

Step 2 – defining and understanding the approach to the compliance program

The question you must be able to answer after completing this step is, *"Why is the approach you choose the right one?"*

There are several aspects to this question. The two most important ones are as follows:

▶ Are you going to use a framework? If yes, which one?

▶ Are you going to use external resources such as consultants or lawyers?

Depending on the regulatory requirements you are facing, the usage of a framework is highly recommended. **Frameworks** define a code of practice and principles that could include processes and policies. They provide objectives and sometimes detailed controls to establish, implement, review, and improve compliance and/or security programs.

There are regulatory requirements for public trading companies (for example, SOX and EU-SOX); for medical companies (for example, US HIPAA); or, depending on the size of the company, accounting regulatory requirements (for example, US GAAP or German HGB) that demand a formalized risk and or auditing management. For these requirements, using a framework such as CoBIT/COSO, ISO 2700X, or ITIL is a great help as it offers a structured approach. The areas you have to consider are defined. Some frameworks offer explicit information on control objectives and possible control activities, helping you save time. Why invent the wheel again if it already exists? Many frameworks help you understand your controls and show whether they behave as expected, based on numbers.

The most important aspect while using frameworks is that you must understand them. You don't have to know every detail, but you must know how they work and how you are supposed to use them.

The next question you must answer is the usage of **external resources**. Proper research is necessary. For example, just because someone is a lawyer doesn't mean that the lawyer will understand the regulatory requirements you are interested in. The same holds true for consultants. Conduct research to find consultants who have prior experience in the area that you are looking for.

On the one hand, using consultants will get you expertise and knowledge at once. At the same time, you also get resources if you are not able to meet the demands from within your company. Another aspect is to use them for specific tasks only such as:

▸ A sounding board for your project, important issues, and challenges, or for critical documentation, such as the financial ones for ROI and TCO

▸ A kick-off team to get management attention and stakeholder buy-in

On the other hand, including good consultants will incur expenses with regard to management and budget. Never underestimate the time you need to manage them. You must be very clear on their scope, otherwise scope creeps may occur. For example, the consultants may find additional areas that must be addressed (by them)! Another aspect to remember is that, for a continuous compliance program, you might require certain skills and knowledge. If only a consultant has them, you must train the company staff or you will always require the help of consultants for the compliance program.

Step 3 – defining and understanding the project structure

The question you must be able to answer after completing the next step is *"How is your project structured?"*

Having confirmed the reason and approach to your compliance program, the next step is to define and plan the project structure.

There are several ways to structure your project. A very basic overview of steps for a compliance project, based on the **plan-do-check-act** (**PDCA**) cycle, is provided in the next diagram. This structure will help you start out with a systematic approach and will allow you to have different starting situations. Maybe, you have already finished the planning phase or just want to improve your existing program. Regardless of the structure, the systematic approach to project management and the topics discussed in the following recipes within this chapter are the most important aspects for your compliance project to succeed.

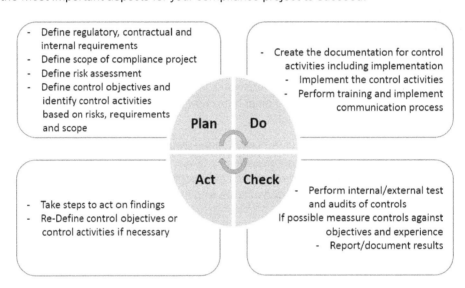

You do not have to create a fully detailed project management plan; however, as shown in the preceding illustration, it should contain the most important stages of the compliance program. These include the resources required for each phase and aspects such as regulatory, contractual, and internal requirements, controls, training, communication, and improvement processes.

How it works...

The reason you must be able to answer the questions in the preceding three steps is that compliance projects lead to changes. Some changes might apply to just one team, but other changes, such as the introduction of a password policy, might affect a large part of your business.

As with every project that introduces changes, there will be opposition to your compliance project. Therefore, you must be able to answer the three questions without hesitation. Otherwise, your project will be dead even before it starts.

▶ `http://www.isaca.org/COBIT/Pages/default.aspx` (the official website for the COBIT framework)

▶ `http://www.iso.org/iso/home/standards.htm` (the official website for the 2700X framework)

▶ `http://www.itil-officialsite.com/` (the official website for the ITIL framework)

▶ `http://www.prince-officialsite.com/` (an example of project management standards/training)

Understanding management support

Before you actually start out with the *do* phase of your compliance project, management support will be key to a successful implementation. The kind of support you require and from whom you require it are the focus of this recipe.

You will not succeed with your systematic compliance program if you do not have true active management support. Whenever possible, involve senior management and business managers in your compliance project.

Getting ready

You must be able to answer the three questions asked in the recipe, *Using project management in your compliance approach*. Without having those answers ready, you should not start with this recipe.

You must always remember that, as with every project, there are few people who will support the compliance program; most people will want to ignore it and some will categorically reject the compliance program. If you do not have answers prepared to face challenges, questions, or issues—for example, why your approach is the best—then the compliance project will lose its credibility, maybe even before it truly ever starts. Challenging questions will come from your business managers and other people within your company.

How to do it...

If you are the person responsible for the compliance program, do not start until you have talked to the CEO or the senior manager who your compliance program is scoped to. If you do not see any other option, use external resources to get the management buy-in by stressing the importance of the project. Ensure they understand, however you do it, that you cannot start the project until you have the support.

The levels of support you require are as follows:

- CEO support or, in the case of a scoped project, the most senior manager responsible for the appropriate unit
- Senior management support in the form of a steering committee or as the actual project team, if your company is small enough
- If the company structure is quite large, the board might have to be involved

The following are examples of the support you require from the CEO or senior manager responsible. As a minimum, the following commitment is required:

- A meeting led by the CEO or senior manager on the compliance strategy to the senior management, or to the essential business leaders you will work with to complete the project
- Gain acceptance on the compliance objectives you defined
- A clear prioritization of your compliance project to the whole business—this also includes the authorization of resources
- Input on whom to include in the steering committee or project team (depending on the size of the company)
- The CEO or senior manager should lead by example by following the changes that will be introduced by the compliance project

You should be prepared to create presentations for meetings held by the CEO or the senior management team, and the presentation on the objectives should be provided by you.

In general, the steering group should include the following members:

- The person responsible for the compliance program
- A member of the legal department
- A senior manager from IT; the largest units affected by the changes, such as operations and sales; and, if possible, training and human resource employees with key functional expertise.

The steering group should be committed to meet regularly for project updates, solving issues and challenges, and serving as a communication channel to the business units, and therefore, the employees.

How it works...

The composition of the steering group or, in smaller companies, the actual project management team, is important. It must include a broad perspective of the company. Thus, a steering group with mainly IT employees is not going to work as compliance is also a business topic, not solely an IT one.

The input of the CEO or senior manager is also important as you have to consider how to integrate or isolate people who reject the compliance project. One possibility to address this issue is to give such managers responsibility for a key aspect of the project.

In the initial meeting of the steering committee, the scope of the project should be defined, the defined objectives should be prioritized, and the next steps planned.

Besides the creation of the steering group, there are several areas within the compliance project where input and support from the CEO or the senior manager is important. The following paragraphs provide some examples. Be aware of these and prepare for them within your project.

Implementing a compliance program is a **change management** project. This means there are going to be changes within your company. Most of them will be low-key changes, such as introducing an Internet usage policy or improving existing processes. However, that is not the key point. There are numerous studies out there that show that employees are not looking forward to any changes in their working environment. Changes always mean insecurities and risks they must cope with. So, as mentioned before, you will face resistance. To overcome them, you require a communication structure, which we will talk about in a later recipe, and you will require the CEO and senior management to live those changes as an example to the rest of the company.

For this reason, management support is required to address the challenges. In order to gain support, you must answer the following questions before you approach your management:

- Why those changes are required, leading to the question, "Why did you choose those control objectives and, if already defined, control activities?"
- What results do you want to achieve, leading to the question, "Why do you think the results are important to address regulatory requirements?"

Another point to remember is that the compliance project will not be the only one in your business. **Project prioritization** must also be considered. This should be done by you with your CEO or Senior Management. Prioritization is also important to overcome resistance, or you will always be in a situation where your project is seriously delayed due to missing resources or resistance from a business manager whose teams might have important input on regulatory requirements. Another aspect of prioritization is the compliance status in the overall company culture. What is more important to your business, compliance or higher sales (by ignoring regulatory requirements)?

The most important aspect is that several control objectives are business-not IT-related, thus making this a **business project** too. Therefore, you require input from the senior management about the business strategy and goals and the business model.

Both aspects must be understood as they have a direct influence on risk assessment, control objectives, and control activities. For example, if the company is planning to offer products not only within the country of your origin but also to another country, different regulatory requirements will apply in the future. If this happens, additional questions arise, for example, *"How do you address different or even conflicting regulatory requirements for those trades?"* To summarize, you must understand the business strategy and understand whether changes are planned, as they have a direct impact on your compliance program.

Defining your communication approach

A working communication process is the next key aspect for the successful implementation of a compliance program. There are two reasons for this. The first one is about the nature of the compliance project. As mentioned in the previous recipe, compliance means change. To gain support not only from your senior management and business managers, but also from the employees affected by those changes, an adequate communication plan must exist or must be implemented prior to starting the project. The other reason is that each employee must be reached to know what is expected of them. If there are changes or additions to policies, a communication strategy must exist to reach the affected users. Keep in mind that you wouldn't need to reach all the users every time you wish to communicate information.

Getting ready

The structure of your project management team and responsibilities must be defined. You must know who is responsible for which business area. This should allow you to communicate the project using the appropriate employees for a given communication. For example, the head of IT will be the best person to communicate the detailed project to the IT team; however, the CEO or head of Human Resources may communicate company-wide changes that are relative to the program.

How to do it...

If there is no communication process established within the company yet, allow time within your project plan to develop one. Your communication plan could include systems such as websites (intranet), telephone conferencing systems, e-mail, and/or chat systems for newsletters and documents (define a standard with regards to format, content, and type of documents) for meetings, reports, and so on.

Depending on your company, decide which system to use for each type of communication. Decide how best to get input or what channels to use for conflict management. For example, providing general information on the compliance program to all the employees within your company might be best done using websites on your intranet. If you know that the intranet is not used by most users but the monthly hard copy newsletter is, then use the latter medium instead.

If a communication platform is established, the communication plan should address at least the following:

- Definition of the steering group and other stakeholder communication objectives
- Responsibilities for providing and writing communications to the targeted groups
- Definition of technologies or methods to convey the given information
- Definition of the frequency of communication
- Definition of the escalation procedures to resolve issues

A very basic communication plan could be as shown in the following table:

Stakeholder or target audience	Type of communication	Person responsible	Objectives	Due date
Steering committee	Meeting	Compliance project manager	Updating on the progress and addressing issues	Every other week
Business managers	Report	Member of the steering committee responsible for the business manager's area	Updating on the progress	Regularly once a month
Employee with key functional expertise	E-mail	Compliance project manager	Asking simple questions	Ad hoc
Internal employee	Website (intranet)	Compliance project manager or a member of the steering committee for responsible business areas or topics	Providing general information on the compliance project, providing online form for feedback	Regular monthly updates Ad hoc
Affected employees	Meeting	Trainer	Training to establish committed behavior	Ad hoc for new topics, conducted once a year
Affected third parties	Reports via mail or hard copy	Compliance project manager	Providing general information on the project and expected changes	Ad hoc when a third party is affected

How it works...

You have to create a top-down approach for your communication strategy. Depending on the target audience, you have to translate the information you want to provide. Some of the information in your initial communication should include answers to the following questions:

- ▶ Why is the compliance project necessary?
- ▶ What are the legal responsibilities that have to be followed?
- ▶ What benefits will it generate for employees at different levels?

As mentioned before, the answer has to be tailored to the group being addressed.

The next step should include regular briefings on the compliance project. Here, you, as the compliance project manager, should address the steering committee and/or the project team. The responsible senior managers should provide the necessary information to their business areas. The communication plan must contain a commitment; the business managers will then provide the necessary information to their teams.

For additional buy-in within your company, you should establish communication processes to include employees with expertise in their areas. For example, in *Chapter 2, Implementing the First Steps of Basic Compliance*, we talked about segregation of duty as a possible control activity. If you have defined that segregation of duty is necessary within operations to comply with a regulatory requirement, schedule a meeting with one or more employees from the affected business units and talk to them about possible approaches and how to best streamline the processes to address the segregation of duty. This will ensure the buy-in of the business unit, as those changes will not be made without their involvement.

Besides direct involvement, you can also provide a mechanism to ensure regular or ad hoc feedback from people within your company. Do not forget to include affected third parties.

Planning the risk assessment approach

This recipe addresses **risk assessment**, including the definition of **risks** and **threats** that will influence your decision on the control objectives and activities you choose. The recipe provides further advice on control selections.

There are several reasons for using a risk assessment approach for your compliance program.

The first reason is already mentioned in recipe 1 step 2. There are several regulatory requirements of which risk assessment is an integral part.

The second reason is that risk assessment allows you to have a systematic approach to your control selection. Risk assessment will make you aware of the kind of risks, threats, and vulnerabilities your company faces with respect to its sensitive data, information systems, employees, and so on. This will provide several advantages to your business. First, you have a better understanding of the true costs of the product you offer. Second, as part of risk assessment, you not only examine the asset, but the relative embedded processes as well. The risk assessment process will optimize processes as errors or inefficiencies are identified and eliminated, leading to fewer errors in the process itself. This means employees will be more proficient.

The third reason is the fulfillment of regulatory requirements that demand risk management as this could lead to better ratings, for example, insurance premiums.

Getting ready

Understand the kind of controls that are already in place in your company. Understand your core business processes.

Work through *Chapter 1, Starting the Compliance Process for Small Businesses,* as this recipe is based on some content from that chapter.

How to do it...

The following diagram provides an overview of the risk analysis process. The goal is to understand the kinds of risks your sensitive information, information systems, buildings, and so on are facing, including the type of damage or possible loss. Based on this information, activities will be defined to handle at least the highest risks to your sensitive assets.

As part of risk assessment, start with the risk analysis by *identifying all assets* within the scope of your compliance program. This could include information in the form of documents, information systems or devices, passwords, employees, and so on. Always use the criterion that an asset is something of value to the business.

Try not to be over-creative or to get into too much detail. It doesn't matter whether there are 10 or 100 servers handling sensitive information. It is just important to understand that they exist and should be considered in your risk assessment plan.

Understanding important assets of your company helps to determine countermeasures in order to protect them using one of the items listed in the treatment plan. As part of asset identification, create a classification of assets. This asset classification will make it much easier to decide on actual controls later on as you do not have to define a control for every asset; rather, you could define the control for the asset class.

Examples could include:

> **Authenticators**: This could include passwords or PINs

> **Sensitive customer data**: This could include any information that must be protected, such as financial data, legal documentation that is not publicly available, and account data

> **Sensitive employee data**: This could include financial data or any information in the HR file

The next phase is to *identify threats* against each asset. A threat is considered to be an event or incident with an undesired impact on your asset. Each threat should be considered for the confidentiality, integrity, and availability of the asset.

You must define the different categories of threats you want to consider. The following list provides some examples:

> **Nature**: This could include things such as flooding, earthquake, fire, and tornadoes

> **Errors and omission**: During data entry, operations, or development, errors or omissions could lead to data leaks, loss of security integrity, and/or system instability

> **Fraud and theft**: This includes systems that hold sensitive information such as your order-processing system

> **Malicious code**: This includes a Trojan, virus, or any other software that does not perform as expected

> **Disclosure**: This includes breach of confidentiality or disclosure of business or customer information

As with identification of assets, do not get carried away with this step. For example, when considering the category "nature", including an earthquake in your threat list is quite unlikely for a northern European country, whereas a flood is likely if your company is close to a river. So, for all different types of threats, only include realistic ones.

Next, you should focus on *identifying all the potential vulnerabilities* that each asset has for each threat. A vulnerability is a flaw or oversight in an existing control that might make it possible for a threat to exploit that vulnerability, for example, to gain unauthorized access.

You should consider different categories. The following list provides examples:

- ▶ **Physical**: For example, technical equipment that is not secured
- ▶ **Technical**: For example, a weak password and misconfigured access points
- ▶ **Nature**: For example, fire and having no second fire protection area or flammable materials in your server room
- ▶ **Personnel**: For example, no background check for highly sensitive positions

The next step should be to *identify the impact* on the identified assets. For each asset, consider the threat and vulnerability and determine what kind of impact will arise from it. A systematic approach to impact analysis should include a risk matrix as shown in the following diagram. The definition of the different categories should be an input for the prioritization of assets with regard to control.

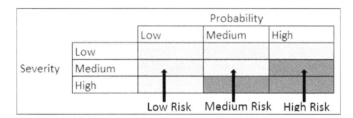

The following table provides examples on how to define probability and severity:

Category	High	Medium	Low
Probability	Incident occurs weekly. Incident occurs at least once every 1000 transactions.	Incident occurs; it does not occur weekly, but more than once a month. Incident occurs at least once every 10,000 transactions.	Incident occurs less than once a month. Incidents occur at least once every 1,000,000 transactions.
Severity	The whole business is impacted. No further work is possible on process XX. The loss by the incident will be at least USD 1,000,000.	A business unit is impacted. Only manual work is possible. The loss by the incident will be at least USD 500,000.	A single person is impacted. No perceivable hindrance. The loss by the incident will be less than USD 500,000.

Everything that belongs to the category of High Risk is not acceptable to the business and must be addressed. Medium Risks should be addressed and Low Risks should be accepted but still monitored.

The risk assessment should be a combination of probability and severity, meaning the likelihood of occurrence and damage or losses the company might face.

As with threat and vulnerability assessment, develop categories for the kind of damage or loss you expect. The type of impact you expect will have an impact on your control selection. Examples of such categories are as follows:

- Business interruption
- Financial losses including fines and penalties or lawsuits
- Reputational loss including loss of customer

The last step will be the selection of appropriate activities to handle the risk identified. So, the risk assessment process provides the input for the *identification of your controls*.

We already talked about the types of controls and control selection in *Chapter 1, Starting the Compliance Process for Small Businesses*. To summarize, the goal of controls is to manage risks through policies, processes, and/or guidelines. The actual implementation could be, for example, technical control (such as logins and passwords) or legal (such as a contract). It must be appropriate. I have seen customers who configure their antivirus systems to scan everything every time a change occurs. This will lead to extremely slow systems and sporadic corruptions. It won't add additional benefits to a more considered approach. It was just a literal interpretation of a control identified within the compliance program. Employees should be trained to understand the controls and impact (as mentioned before, communication is key).

After you complete the risk assessment, you might have to reconsider controls that have been implemented prior to it. Those controls probably do not meet your criteria for accepting the risks we mentioned in the *How it works...* section of this recipe. Additionally, to answer the question *"What do you not know yet?"*, different control activities could be implemented to gain answers to questions such as the following:

- Do critical assets reside on systems that are compliant with your company security standards or do they reside on systems reviewed for physical security?
- Is the company prepared to handle the compromise of critical assets? For example, after measuring the compromised assets in terms of percentage or a number (something like *n* out of 100 assets), does the company have a documented risk mitigation plan for those assets?

The last thing to remember is that risk assessment is a recurring step; your company's strategy changes and your business operation changes. This must be reflected in your risk assessment and, therefore, your controls.

How it works...

As mentioned throughout this book, keep in mind that compliance is not just IT, but also a business topic. For realistic risk assessment, management input is required. Some examples that influence your risk assessment were mentioned in the recipe *Understanding management support*. Another example is the understanding of how risk-averse your company is. For example, when faced with introducing a new product, is it OK to go ahead with a less secure but faster implementation and, maybe, a less expensive one instead of a more time-consuming and expensive but more secure implementation? Another example would be if your company undertakes an annual penetration test for its public-facing websites, but only addresses the top five identified risks; a more risk-averse company may seek to remediate all risks or clearly document those that pose no threat. In other words, the goal is to define the criteria for accepting risks and identifying the level of risk your company will accept.

One criterion could be that the company will accept any risk where the economic impact is less than the cost of controlling it. When we say the cost of controlling, it includes not only the value of the information or system affected by the risk, but also the surrounding costs of the control, such as hardware cost, process cost, and so on.

Risk management examines the probability of a negative incident that will *only* incur a loss for the company or prevent something desirable from happening. It never leads to opportunities.

Risk management includes activities to address them. The most commons ones are as follows:

- Eliminating the risk
- Reducing a risk that cannot be eliminated to an acceptable level within acceptable means
- Accepting the risk
- Transferring the risk through insurance, outsourcing, contracts, or other means

Many companies use confidentiality, integrity, and availability when looking at specific risks within the risk assessment process.

The goal of risk assessment should be to answer the question, *"What do you not know about your company landscape with regard to sensitive information and regulatory requirements?"* Answering this question will allow you to identify potential areas not addressed in your company that affect the organization's most critical information or systems.

There's more...

As mentioned before, frameworks provide exhaustive lists of risks, threats, vulnerabilities, and controls to address those. Therefore, you do not have to invent everything on your own. Using one of the frameworks could help save time. For example, ISO 27005 provides a risk management framework.

Another great help for compliance projects is initiatives that help you with the selection of control objectives and control activities. **Unified Compliance Frameworks** (**UCF**) is one of those initiatives that takes apart thousands of local and international laws, industry standards, and frameworks and extracts the requirements. These requirements are then translated into control objectives and activities. The benefit is that these control objectives and control activities are unified. Quite often, different laws or industry standards demand the same but the wording is different. The UCF provides an overview of correlation between them. This will be a great time saver as you can at once see which requirements demand the same controls and are able to prevent the implementation of different controls for different laws but for the same requirement.

Planning documentation requirements

The goal of this recipe is to provide advice on considerations for documentation and reports. Documentation is seen by many as a waste of time; however, for the compliance project, it is one of the key aspects to succeed.

Getting ready

To work with this recipe, you just need passion to succeed with this project.

How to do it...

There are different kinds of documents you have to create. The following list provides an overview of the most important ones:

- Policies
- Training documents
- Testing and/or auditing documents

Policies must be available for different hierarchical levels within your company, with a different focus on each level. Examples of the different kinds of levels and their intent or target are as follows:

- An overall policy provided by senior management to define the company's compliance culture

- ▶ A policy that details the control, how it is implemented, the business process this control is used in, the regulatory requirements met by this control, and similar content

- ▶ A policy that focuses on the employees responsible for providing and/or operating the control

- ▶ A policy with focus on employees who have to adhere to the controls

A brief overview of the format for the last two types of policies will be provided in the following list. As stated in *Chapter 1*, *Starting the Compliance Process for Small Businesses*, while planning the compliance process for small businesses, many data protection laws or the standard PCI DSS demand access controls. To comply with this requirement, introducing a password policy and segregation of duty for more sensitive system might be required. In this case, the policy—let's call it "Access Control Policy"—will address the employee group that must implement, operate, and provide input for tests (optionally). So the format of this policy could be as follows:

- ▶ General information on the policy that includes the following:
  - ❑ The purpose of the document
  - ❑ Cross-reference to other documents that might apply
  - ❑ Scope detailing for the systems, application, and employees this policy is applicable to

- ▶ An Access Control process that includes the following:
  - ❑ An explanation of why this is important—what goals the company wants to achieve. For example, user accounts require passwords for authentication to prevent the account from being shared and shared passwords from being used
  - ❑ Information on requirements and preventive controls with the focus on systems, for example, the minimum required password complexity and rules on password storage (that is, the system should never store passwords in clear text)
  - ❑ The optimal solution that should be implemented for certain systems, such as multifactor authentication
  - ❑ Information on preventive controls for user behavior, such as limiting the number of login attempts or how to deal with unattended sessions
  - ❑ The process for exemption if the listed requirements cannot be met

- ▶ Review the requirements of the controls that include the following:
  - ❑ Definition of the kind of review required for the control, for example, monthly reviews to ensure that accounts are deleted/disabled for employees who left the company or changed their business unit
  - ❑ This section could include sample sizing, minimum schedule, responsibilities, and the goal of the review

In comparison, the policy for the employee who has to work with the systems affected by Access Control Policy will be much less detailed. This policy might only include the following:

- General information on the policy that includes the following:
    - The purpose of the document
    - Cross-referencing other documents that might apply
    - Scope detailing for the systems, application, and employees this policy is applicable to

- The purpose of the policy:
    - An explanation of why this is important
    - Details about the Password Policy complexity that the user must be aware of when changing his or her passwords

Training documents come in different formats too; some are more formal for new employees to make them understand what is expected of them. Sometimes, the last policy mentioned in the list is used. However, this isn't a good approach, as you will have several policies, and employees might not read them if you just hand them out a big pile of paper. To make them attractive to the employees, different formats should be used. This could include PowerPoint presentations shown during training events, online forms (as games) for self-study, or hands-on training.

Work hard to get a training slot on the initial day for new employees; 30 minutes is a great starting point to make your pitch for a compliant "code of conduct" and convey how important this topic is within the business. Equally important is the ongoing annual training program.

How it works...

Documentation is important for different reasons. The first is about consistency. You need the documentation as a kind of reference. You have to document the risk management process and the controls selected. Without documenting the risk management or control selection process, you will have to restart this part whenever a review of the adequacy of your controls is scheduled. If you do not have any documentation, how will you know whether the current controls are adequate?

Creating documentation standards for your compliance program will ensure that a consistent approach to all of the content is used across your whole environment. Based on compliance decisions you make, good documentation will enable you to create clear policies and guidelines that will ensure that the decision made will be understood and adhered to by the whole company consistently.

The second is about accountability. Especially with regard to risk management and a decision for or against certain controls, a documented approach is necessary. You have to be able to explain why you made certain decisions to auditors or management. In addition, many laws and standards, such as data protection laws, tax laws, and standards in finance or medicine, demand documented controls and especially proof of effective controls. This means you have to perform periodic reviews and the results, and your subsequent actions based on those results, must be documented.

System Center tools help with these requirements. Automated controls within the System Center tools have an automatic log. Regular reports will provide documentation on controls, please see *Chapter 9, Reporting on Compliance with Microsoft System Center 2012*, for further information.

The next recipe will provide more information on testing.

Defining your test approach

This recipe focuses on answering the question about the effectiveness of your compliance program. You must perform periodic tests to determine whether your control objectives are truly met by the controls you implemented. If there is a problem that appears again and again in your test, you should know that you must redesign it. Without periodic tests, you will never be able to find the problems.

It is just like traffic; everyone sees the speed limit signs but, without periodic controls by the police, many people would simply ignore them, even though we know that driving above the speed limit could lead to undesired consequences.

Getting ready

You must have your controls documented and truly understand the goals you try to achieve. In addition, you must know the risks your company is willing to accept.

How to do it...

The following illustration provides an example of the process and the steps required while conducting compliance tests:

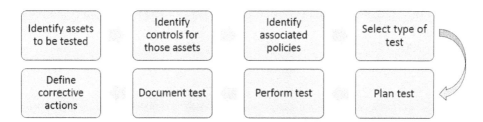

The diagram is explained as follows:

1. Decide on the assets to be included in your test. The decision on what to include should consider the regulatory requirement (some demand certain schedules), the probability of fraud, damage, how error-prone it is, information sensitivity, input/output flow, and past audit findings.

2. Identify the associated controls. In this step, you require the documentation we mentioned in the previous recipe. Looking at our example introduced in *Chapter 1, Starting the Compliance Process for Small Businesses*, we should ask which control ensures that information entered into the order-processing system is valid and that the resulting orders are valid. In this case, we will find a mandated access control.

3. We know the control we are looking for is access control. So we know that we require the Access Control policy. The access control policy determines the expected behavior. In our case, we have asked for a password requirement with a certain password complexity. In addition to this, we have asked for segregation of duty. We might have stated a requirement that no employee be able to authorize an order above a certain amount. Instead, the four-eye principle should be used. The expected outcome of the test, based on the policy, could be password complexity and segregation of duty for orders above a certain amount.

4. Depending on the control, different methods might be used. Most commonly, this includes looking at documentations, application status or other sources, interviews of employees, or observing the employees while they are performing the process.

5. The type of tests depends on the control. For automatic controls, sampling is the most useful method, as each automated control must have a log (preferably one that cannot be manipulated or is very hard to manipulate).

6. Planning includes several steps, such as selecting the sample size to test. This should reflect the importance of the asset for a process or data flow, severity of fraud, damage, errors that might arise from this asset (if this value can be defined), number of changes to the process this asset resides in or changes to the asset itself, and the complexity of the asset. It must include who is responsible for the overview of the test and who will conduct the test. It is quite important to define how the test should be done. The last thing to define is the minimum schedule for this test. In the example for "access control," a monthly review should be done to ensure that people who leave the company should not have any active accounts left. Samples should be provided by HR (employees that left the company the previous month) and should be tested against a randomly tested information system that is most critical to the business and that the employee had worked with. The tester could be the system owner (here IT or helpdesk) and the person responsible for the test could be from the compliance team.

7. This step is straightforward as everything detailed in step 6 must be performed.

8. The resulting documentation should include what has been tested, who was involved, and the results. In the case of sensitive information (as in the previous example), documentation of the percentage or number of successful tests and error tests should be made. For example, on Application XX, 10 accounts out of 30 accounts were deactivated; on Application XX, 30 accounts of 30 accounts were deleted; and so on.

9. Depending on the assets and their sensitivity to the frequency of occurrence of failed test results, action might have to be taken. Based on the documentation of the results, try to determine the cause of the failed test and the significance of the result. Is it a minor problem, or will the continued occurrence lead to financial loss, reputational loss, and so on?

How it works...

Creating a testing plan and testing it are fairly straightforward. First, you must decide the kinds of tests you will use, governed by regulatory, contractual, or internal requirements. Some laws or industry standards may demand a certain format and schedule for your tests.

Look at all the requirements you have and create an overall schedule for your tests. The schedule will include regular tests that might be carried out on a weekly, monthly, quarterly, or yearly basis. In addition, periodically run a more thorough test and review of controls (targeting sensitive assets) to ensure that they are up-to-date and remain adequate. Often, these additional, in-depth tests are done by internal auditor for everything that they are not responsible for.

6
Planning a Compliance Program in Microsoft System Center 2012

In this chapter, we will cover the following topics:

- Understanding the responsibilities of the System Center 2012 tools
- Planning the implementation of Microsoft System Center 2012 Service Manager
- Planning the connection of the System Center 2012 components
- Planning and defining the responsibilities for a compliance program
- Planning System Center Service Manager 2012 related settings and configuration
- Planning and defining compliance reports

Introduction

Depending on the goal of your control objectives, therefore control activities, different technical tools may be required to achieve them. Which tool to use and how everything fits together will be the focus of the recipes in this chapter.

After starting with the planning of an enterprise-focused compliance project, one important aspect is the tool selection and technical implementation of your compliance project. The following two aspects have to be remembered:

- No tool exists that will magically run your compliance process and solve all your compliance problems
- No tools exist that will fit your company and processes 100%

The tools and technologies are important as they can help you create a cost-effective and efficient compliance process and support other aspects such as risk assessment and management. Still, they are only a *means* to your goal and not the solution.

Each tool has strengths, but also some gaps. In addition, only you can understand your business; for example, how risk averse your company is or what the company strategy for the future is. Maybe the company plans to outsource different processes. That would mean different compliance requirements.

Many books on **Governance Risk and Compliance** (**GRC**) or standard frameworks, such as ITIL, define a planning process that does not include actual tool considerations. The goal is to allow the creation of a compliance program optimized for the company's business requirements based on the business processes and goals.

In theory this is a great idea, but practically it will lead to additional costs, frustration, and sometimes, failure of the project. Several times I have seen companies create a great planning phase with risk assessment and controls to address those risks. Unfortunately, during the implementation phase, no tool was found that could reproduce the desired control and documentation requirements. Either a tool for just a given control was introduced or expensive additions to an existing tool were made. Most often, the result is a control that is not consistent with the risk associated. Always keep in mind that your compliance program, especially your control activities and reports, have to be run regularly and should be proportional to the targeted risk they try to address.

This chapter will provide information on steps to determine which tools to use. The focus is on controls and reports realized via System Center products. The System Center family is a data center management suite with each tool focusing on certain areas of it. Together, they provide the most comprehensive and integrated suite for datacenter management. Each of the tools includes compliance aspects sufficient for audit requirements. The planning prerequisites, compliance aspects covered by the tools, and how they fit together will be the focus of the following recipes.

Understanding the responsibilities of the System Center 2012 tools

This recipe shows how the System Center tools, in addition to Security Compliance Manager, work together and it also explains the focus of each tool.

Getting ready

In order to create a successful compliance program, you must have a clear understanding of your goals and regulatory and business requirements. This information is key in understanding which control objectives are required and which control activities fulfill your goals and requirements, that is, your control objectives. You should have already worked through *Chapter 1*, *Starting the Compliance Process for Small Businesses* and *Chapter 5*, *Starting an Enterprise Compliance Program*.

How to do it...

Based on your company and regulatory requirements, you must create your control objectives. As mentioned in *Chapter 5*, *Starting an Enterprise Compliance Program*, there are libraries, such as the **Unified Compliance Framework** (**UCF**), that provide control objectives and control activities based on regulatory requirements such as privacy laws and frameworks such as **COBIT**, **COSO**, and so on. These compliance libraries are great tools to help you with this first step, but always keep in mind that they are just tools.

The following diagram provides a visual summary of the tasks required for the successful creation of a technical compliance program showing which System Center tool to use for the different tasks. The tasks are as follows:

- ▸ Define compliance requirements
- ▸ Perform authorized implementation
- ▸ Review adherence to compliance requirements
- ▸ Perform remediation

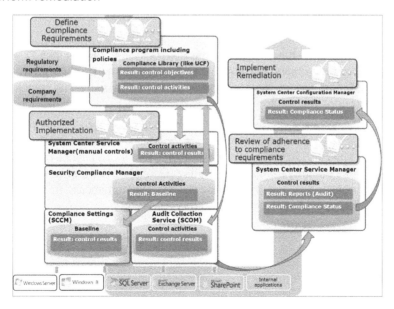

The minimum steps that are required are as follows:

1. Define and document your compliance program, including compliance policies, standards, corresponding control objectives, and control activities. The results of this step are control objectives and control activities.

    Based on the scenario of access compliance, you should create a password policy that states the password rules and the reasons for the policy. This must be distributed to your users.

    With your policy and, more importantly, regulatory and company requirements in mind, decide on your control activities.

2. The results of step 1 are the input for this task—for manual controls, use **System Center Service Manager** for documentation. The results are control status information.

    Based on the password policy scenario, in case no System Center Configuration Manager exists, the correct implementation of password policy would have to be checked manually. The result of this check should be entered into **System Center Service Manager**. This could either be entered in Incident or Change Management. Creating either one provides a record of the manual control and has the benefit of being included in the System Center Service Manager reports.

3. The results of step 1 are the input for this task—for automated control activities based on configuration settings do the following:

    1. Use **Security Compliance Manager** to create compliance baselines for control activities of configuration settings. The result is the compliance baseline.

        Based on the password policy scenario, as described in *Chapter 2, Implementing the First Steps of Basic Compliance*, create a baseline with your password policy.

    2. The input is the compliance baseline from the previous step. Use **Compliance Settings** within **System Center Configuration Manager** to run the compliance baseline. The results are compliance control status information.

        Based on the password policy scenario, as described in *Chapter 3, Enhancing the Basic Compliance Program Using Microsoft System Center 2012 Configuration Manager*, use the compliance baseline from **Security Compliance Manager** to ensure adherence to it. After configuring the controls, those will be run automatically. In addition, auto-remediation of failed controls is possible.

4. The results of step 1 are inputs for this task—for automated control activities based on breach status, use **Audit Collection Services** from **System Center Operations Manager**. The results are compliance breach information.

   Based on the password policy scenario, create a monitoring rule for unauthorized access to critical systems and unauthorized changes to your password policy.

5. The results from steps 2, 3, and 4 are input for compliance status and audit reports. Reports are available in the following:

   1. System Center Service Manager for manual control activities. In addition to centralized reports of automated controls, where input of the controls comes from other tools such as System Center Configuration Manager. The reports are based on the System Center Service Manager function of Incident or Change Management.

   2. System Center Configuration Manager for control activities in the previous step 3.

   3. System Center Operations Manager for control activities in step 4.

6. The results from step 3 could be remediated automatically. The results of steps 2 and 4 must be considered and, if required, steps for remediation should be taken.

How it works...

The tool to use for control objectives and the corresponding control activities depends on the possible input and the required result of the control activity. The most basic questions that have to be answered are as follows:

▶ Does the control activity have a manual input/output?

▶ Is the control activity based on a query for system or application configuration status information?

▶ Is the control activity based on a query for monitoring/breaching status information?

▶ What type of control (manual or automated) and which characteristic of the control (preventive or detective) do you require?

Based on the answers to those questions, it is possible to understand which System Center tool or Microsoft technology to use. The following table illustrates this:

Type of control objectives / control activities	Details/examples	System Center product
Manual control	Manual activities must be performed. Results must be entered into a system manually.	System Center Service Manager
Automated control based on configuration status	Input based on Active Directory or registry settings to prevent risks from occurring	Security Compliance Manager in addition to System Center Configuration Manager
Characteristic: Preventive or detective	Input based on application or system settings to prevent risk from occurring	System Center Configuration Manager
	Reports to monitor configuration status, for example, of Active Directory password settings to detect non-compliance	System Center Configuration Manager or System Center Service Manager
Automated control based on monitoring/ breach status Characteristic: Detective	Input based on monitoring of logs or compliance breach status information	System Center Operations Manager

Creating automated control activities within the System Center tools is but one task. The next steps must be as follows:

- Creating notifications or alerts for relevant stakeholders and reports
- Performing remediation

Every System Center tool has its own reporting capability. This means there are different compliance reports in different System Center tools. To enhance usability, System Center Service Manager could be used to centralize most of those reports.

Remediation for automated control activities, based on configuration settings, is the feature of System Center Configuration Manager. Depending on the requirements, after running a control activity compliance baseline that includes storing the results, all negative results of control activities could be remediated automatically, as shown in *Chapter 3, Enhancing the Basic Compliance Program Using Microsoft System Center 2012 Configuration Manager*. For auto-remediation based on monitoring or breach information, System Center Configuration Manager offers the capability to define actions. System Center Operations Manager offers the same capabilities.

Each breach of a baseline could be auto-remediated out of the box. Regardless of the tool used, remediation must always be done in a documented fashion as this is a very common compliance requirement. In case a change is involved, the change management capabilities of System Center Service Manager should be used. All System Center tools create logs showing the action performed.

There's more...

Besides the already mentioned System Center tools, there are two more tools that belong to the core System Center product family. These are System Center Virtual Machine Manager and System Center Data Protection Manager.

System Center 2012 R2 Virtual Machine Manager doesn't offer any compliance functionalities. It includes an audit log of administrator activities. This is a requirement in several regulatory requirements and therefore is quite useful. Out of the box, no additional benefits are provided.

System Center 2012 R2 Data Protection Manager (**SCDPM**) is different. This tool is used for Backup and Disaster Recovery. These two topics are requirements in many standards and regulatory requirements. But there are already great books out there focusing on SCDPM, such as the following one:

```
http://www.amazon.com/Microsoft-System-Center-Protection-Manager/
dp/1849686300/ref=sr_1_1?ie=UTF8&qid=1403700777&sr=8-1&keywords=Syste
m+Center+Data+Protection+Manager
```

Therefore, we have not included any recipes of SCDPM in this book.

See also

- ► `http://technet.microsoft.com/en-us/library/gg681958.aspx` (the article in the Technet library on the planning of Compliance Settings in SCCM 2012)
- ► `http://technet.microsoft.com/en-us/library/hh212740.aspx` (planning of Audit Collection Service in SCOM 2012 in the Technet library)
- ► `http://technet.microsoft.com/en-us/solutionaccelerators/cc835245.aspx` (the article in the Technet library on the planning of compliance baselines in Security Compliance Manager)

Planning the implementation of Microsoft System Center 2012 Service Manager

Microsoft's **System Center 2012 Service Manager** (**SCSM 2012**) can be used to manage IT management processes (ITIL and MOF). The compliance management process is related to the IT management processes as well.

Compliance issues can be handled as incident records; also, compliance related changes can be managed in SCSM 2012 as Change Requests.

Getting ready

Before we start planning the installation of SCSM 2012, you should be familiar with the ITIL or MOF management processes.

Also, you should have planned the Incident and Change Management process for IT.

How to do it...

An example of the steps to plan the installation of the SCSM 2012 environment is as follows:

1. Identify the required components of SCSM 2012. The SP1 or R2 version are also suitable.
2. Identify the sizing of the SCSM 2012 infrastructure.
3. Identify the amount of Configuration Items you want to have in the CMDB of SCSM 2012.

How it works...

The different components available in SCSM 2012 are shown in the following table:

Component	Required	Function
SCSM 2012 Management Server	Yes	The SCSM 2012 Management Server is the main part of a SCSM environment. The management server will manage all Configuration Items and Work Items and is responsible for all workflows as well. You need at least one Management Server in each SCSM 2012 environment.
SCSM 2012 Data Warehouse Server	Yes	The SCSM 2012 Data Warehouse Server offers reports and cubes to analyze and report on SCSM 2012 objects.
SCSM 2012 Self-Service Portal	Optional	A web-based interface for the end user. For the compliance process, Self-Service is not needed mandatorily.

For good performance in SCSM 2012, sizing and planning of the environment is essential. There is a Service Manager Sizing Helper tool available in the Service Manager job that aids documentation. You can download the `SM_job_aids.zip` file at `http://go.microsoft.com/fwlink/p/?LinkID=232378`.

One sizing related factor is the amount of managed **Configuration Items** (**CIs**), for instance, managed users, computers, groups, printers, and other IT-related objects. Planning the numbers of CIs influences the sizing of the SCSM 2012 as well.

There's more...

The **IT Governance, Risk and Compliance Management Pack** (**IT GRC MP**) is not supported in SCSM 2012 R2. The last supported version is the Microsoft System Center 2012 SP1 Service Manager.

See also

- `http://www.itil-officialsite.com/` (IT Infrastructure Library)
- `http://technet.microsoft.com/en-us/library/cc543224.aspx` (Microsoft Operations Framework)
- `http://technet.microsoft.com/en-us/library/hh519640.aspx` (planning of SCSM 2012 in the Technet library)
- `http://www.packtpub.com/microsoft-system-center-service-manager-2012-cookbook/book` (*Microsoft System Center 2012 Service Manager Cookbook*)
- `http://www.microsoft.com/en-us/download/details.aspx?id=4953` (IT GRC Process Management Pack SP1 for System Center Service Manager)

Planning the connection of the System Center 2012 components

Many components of the System Center 2012 suite are related to each other and can exchange and share information with each other. Also, other IT components such as Microsoft Active Directory can synchronize information with SCSM 2012 (for instance, users and computer information). All CIs are stored in the **Configuration Management Database** (**CMDB**) in System Center 2012 Service Manager.

Getting ready

Before you plan the connections of the System Center 2012 components and Active Directory, you should identify the compliance-management-related IT items.

Based on the different requirements of regulatory documents, the required and related items may vary.

How to do it...

To manage compliance issues in SCSM 2012, you have to plan the related CIs that are needed in the CMDB.

The following CI object classes are available by default in SCSM 2012:

CI object class	Function
Users	All users with user-related attributes; for instance, first name, last name, phone number, and e-mail address
Computers	All computer objects with related attributes; for instance, the computer name and domain
Groups	All groups with related attributes; for instance, the group name and domain
Printers	All printers with related attributes; for instance, the printer name

Plan and define additional CI object classes in SCSM 2012. Additional CI classes could be as follows:

- ▶ Network components
- ▶ Databases
- ▶ IT Services
- ▶ Facility components

To get all the information and attributes of CIs in the SCSM 2012 CMDB, planning of connectors to other System Center components is needed. Also, any manual input of CIs should be considered.

An example of the steps to plan the connectors and import of data is as follows:

- ▶ In which IT system is the information stored?
- ▶ Is there a connector to SCSM 2012 available to synchronize the data?
- ▶ What synchronization interval is appropriate for the SCSM 2012 connector?

- ▶ Who is responsible for the correctness and actuality of the data?
- ▶ Is the data available for import in a CSV-formatted file?

How it works...

CIs are stored in the SCSM 2012 CMDB. This way, it is possible in SCSM to store relationships between CIs and Incident Records and other Work Item types.

This offers the opportunity to get all the details and attributes of affected CIs within a compliance-management-related Incident Record or Change Request.

Also, for report and audit purposes, the information stored on the related and affected CIs is required and helpful.

If CI classes that are not in SCSM 2012 are needed, by default, it is possible to add these classes by creating new classes in the SCSM 2012 Authoring tool or by importing System Center 2012 Operations Manager Management Packs.

To synchronize CIs in SCSM 2012, connectors are used. The following list of connectors is available:

Connector	Function
AD connector	Synchronizing user, computer, group, and printer objects and their attributes from AD in SCSM 2012
SCCM connector	Synchronizing hardware and software information from SCCM in SCSM 2012
SCOM connector	Synchronizing CI and Alert information from SCOM 2012 in SCSM 2012
SCVMM connector	Synchronizing information from SCVMM 2012 in SCSM 2012
Orchestrator connector	Synchronizing information of runbooks from Microsoft System Center 2012 Orchestrator in SCSM 2012

To manually import and synchronize information in SCSM 2012, the CSV Import can be used.

There's more...

Many tools provide additional formats for input. The most common one is described in the following section.

Automating CSV import

The import of CSV files can be automated with a workflow or a Scheduled Task. A description of how to automate the CSV import can be found at `http://blogs.technet.com/b/servicemanager/archive/2010/09/24/importing-computers-via-csv.aspx`.

See also

- http://technet.microsoft.com/en-us/library/hh524326.aspx (the *Using Connectors to Import Data into System Center 2012 – Service Manager* article in the Technet library)

- http://www.packtpub.com/microsoft-system-center-service-manager-2012-cookbook/book (*Microsoft System Center 2012 Service Manager Cookbook*)

- http://blogs.technet.com/b/servicemanager/archive/2010/09/27/demo-video-how-to-extend-the-data-model-in-scsm-using-the-authoring-tool.aspx (*Demo Video: How to Extend the Data Model in SCSM Using the Authoring Tool*)

- http://technet.microsoft.com/en-us/library/hh519814.aspx (the *Using a CSV File to Import Data into Service Manager in the Technet Library* article)

Planning and defining the responsibilities for a compliance program

As discussed in *Chapter 5, Starting an Enterprise Compliance Program*, to ensure a successful compliance project, each of the different stakeholders must be included. Stakeholders provide input for the compliance program, such as knowledge on compliance requirements, meaningful control objectives, and activities in addition to support. This recipe will show which stakeholders should be included and what involvement or responsibilities will be required of them within it. The focus of this recipe is to define responsibilities and use the System Center products to realize your compliance program.

Identifying or defining the stakeholder or owner of certain parts of your compliance program at all levels will assist in developing a communication plan at each of those levels. As mentioned in *Chapter 5, Starting an Enterprise Compliance Program*, communication is one of the key steps for the successful implementation of your compliance program.

Getting ready

You should have worked through *Chapter 5, Starting an Enterprise Compliance Program*, successfully. For example, as a minimum, you must be aware of the scope of your compliance project, including locations, assets, and technology.

How to do it...

There are several areas within an organization from which stakeholders must be identified. These areas depend on the business structure and will be different from this example. But as a general guideline, stakeholders from the following levels must be included:

- CEO, COO, and board managers
- Chief Information Security Officer (CISO)
- Compliance and IT Security teams including, if applicable, the audit and compliance team, Risk Officer, IT Security team, and teams/leaders responsible for certain regulatory requirements that overlap with general compliances such as SOX, PCI, or similar
- Business (application) owner
- IT application owner

The types of stakeholders that we will focus on are the last three. It is important to understand who is responsible and the associated responsibilities. In order to place the correct controls, perform them, and, if needed, remediate/change them, this understanding is required. At least the following questions should be asked:

- Who is responsible for your objectives and therefore, your controls?
- Who has to do what?
- What are the required actions?
  - Under what conditions do those actions have to be performed?
  - How do those actions have to be performed?

An example is provided in the following table:

Role of stakeholder	Responsibility	Actions
Compliance team / internal audit	Support the business to address, escalate, and help assess controls	- Perform audit of controls - Escalate remediation of compliance status
Regulatory requirement owner (for example, PCI)	Coordinate alignment of control objectives and activities— if applicable, mapping of compliance processes and PCI processes	- Support the project from a PCI perspective - Assist in communication and escalation - Assist in identification of owners for control activities

Role of stakeholder	Responsibility	Actions
Business owner	▶ Accountability for management of control objectives ▶ Delegates responsibilities and accountability	▶ Support project from the business process owner's perspective ▶ Assist in communication and escalation ▶ Oversee minimum compliance requirements
Business application owner	▶ Gives input for control activities based on control objectives including classification, risk assessment, and risk treatment (which lead to control activities) ▶ Ongoing audit of controls unless done by the compliance team / audit	▶ Identify objectives with regard to compliance requirements
IT application owner	Ensure adherence to compliance policies such as a Password Policy	▶ Perform control activities for the responsible application ▶ Remediate negative compliance status when required

How it works...

The following sections detail the compliance process with focus on connecting the responsibilities to the stakeholder.

Responsibility – primary owner of the overall compliance baseline

In our scenario for password policy, the compliance team would be the primary owner of the compliance baseline. They would ensure that the overall compliance program is started, implemented, and enforced. In this case, they would make sure that the control activities are run as defined. To ensure this, they would either use the System Center Configuration Manager compliance settings report or use System Center Service Manager Incident Management Reports on password policy related incidents.

Responsibility – primary owner for remediation in case of noncompliance

In case one of the control activities reports a security breach, the compliance team will not perform any remediation. This is the responsibility of the IT application owner or a different delegated group.

With regard to a documented (and automatic) remediation, you have to align the IT application owner that would remediate a security breach with Incident Support Group in System Center Service Manager.

In case the control activity for your password policy shows a security breach, the IT application owner for Active Directory or the application affected would be the primary owner to remediate the breach. As we use System Center Configuration Manager as the basis for an automatic control activity and System Center Service Manager for an automatic alert to a breach, the Active Directory Group will be assigned within System Center Service Manager to react to password policy breach alerts. These alerts might come from System Center Operations Manager too. Therefore, use System Center Service Manager to centralize your incident management and the remediation starting point.

At the same time as the assigned group is notified, you should create a workflow within System Center Service Manager to send the owner, via mail or other means, a report of the compliance status. Depending on the criticality, it might be sufficient to send a regular report for information or, in case of a critical breach, a report after the incident has occurred.

Responsibility – primary owner for controls

So far, we have only talked about defining stakeholders/owners with focus on remediation of compliance issues and breaches. Another aspect is compliance program changes.

The compliance team may realize that certain controls have a high noncompliance percentage or that business processes have changed but no reevaluation of controls have been made. For example, in case the password policy no longer meets the business requirements, the following changes may have to be made at several places:

- Documentation has to be updated
- The changes have to be communicated to users and control owners
- The Security Compliance baseline has to be updated
- The new compliance baseline has to be implemented into System Center Configuration Manager

As the primary owner for the overall compliance baseline, the compliance team in our example should work along with the primary owner of these controls; in this case, the business owner.

In order to remain compliant, changes should be documented and traceable in case enquiries are made. Just as for the remediation of compliance issues and security breaches, knowing who is responsible is key in making successful changes to your compliance program. As IT application owners could be defined as support groups within System Center Service Manager, using the Change Management feature will allow you to implement and track changes.

Planning System Center Service Manager 2012 related settings and configuration

In SCSM 2012, it is possible to route and transfer Incident Records to related and responsible support teams or persons. For this reason, it is recommended to plan the classification, the responsible support groups/persons, and prioritization for the Incident Management and for the Change Management process. This will also help with reporting and compliance audits.

Getting ready

Before we start planning the installation of SCSM 2012, you should be familiar with the ITIL and MOF management processes.

Also, you should have planned the Incident and Change Management process for your IT. You should have worked through the previous recipe, *Planning and defining the responsibilities for a compliance program*, to determine the relevant support teams (as primary owners for the different responsibilities) and persons.

How to do it...

For routing and reporting of compliance-related work items, the following information and attributes in SCSM 2012 need to be planned:

- Incident Classification Category (top and child levels)
- Incident Support Groups (groups or persons who are responsible for compliance issues)
- Change Request Area
- Activities in Change Management that are needed for compliance-related Change Requests (Manual and Review Activities)
- Prioritization of compliance-related incidents and change requests

For further use, we will define the following information.

Incident Classification Category is the first one you have to define:

Category (top level)	Category (first child level)	Use of category
Compliance Issue		Generic Incident Classification Category
Compliance Issue	System Security	All compliance issues that are related to System Security; for instance, password policy and access policy
Compliance Issue	Facility	All compliance issues that are related to facility objects; for instance, access control of data centers
Compliance Issue	Perimeter Security	All compliance issues that are related to network security; for instance, network encryption, firewalls, and network intrusion detection
Compliance Issue	Data Privacy	All compliance issues that are related to data privacy; for instance, unauthorized data access

Incident Support Groups/persons are planned and defined in the recipe, *Planning and defining the responsibilities for a compliance program*.

Change Request Area is the next group you have to define:

Area (top level)	Area (first child level)	Use of area
Compliance		Generic Incident Classification Category
Compliance	System Security	All compliance change requests that are related to System Security; for instance, password policy and access policy
Compliance	Facility	All compliance change requests that are related to facility objects; for instance, access control of data centers
Compliance	Network Security	All compliance requests that are related to network security; for instance network encryption
Compliance	Data Privacy	All compliance requests that are related to data privacy; for instance unauthorized data access

After the Incident Classification Categories and Change Request Areas are planned and defined, the next planning step should cover the prioritization of these work items.

The priority is calculated automatically in SCSM 2012 by two factors, namely impact and urgency. The following table can be used for the planning:

Category/Area (top level)	Category/Area (first child level)	Impact	Urgency	Priority (calculated in SCSM)
Compliance Issue		Medium	Medium	3
Compliance Issue	System Security	Medium	High	2
Compliance Issue	Facility	Medium	Medium	3
Compliance Issue	Network Security	Medium	High	2
Compliance Issue	Data Privacy	High	High	1

How it works...

Based on the Incident Classification Categories and Change Request Area, the work item can be transferred to the defined and responsible support group or person.

Defined priorities allow you to focus on the important and critical compliance issues first.

For reporting and later audits, the incident records and change requests can be filtered by the classification category or area.

There's more...

If Incidents and Change Requests occur frequently, the use of templates is valuable. Templates in SCSM 2012 are used to speed up the creation of Work Items and provide a way to standardize the information in them. For instance, there are prefilled **Title** and **Description** fields and a preselected **Category**.

See also

- http://technet.microsoft.com/en-us/library/hh519640.aspx (planning of SCSM 2012 in the Technet library)

- http://www.itil-officialsite.com/ (IT Infrastructure Library)

- http://technet.microsoft.com/en-us/library/cc543224.aspx (Microsoft Operations Framework)

- http://www.packtpub.com/microsoft-system-center-service-manager-2012-cookbook/book (*Microsoft System Center 2012 Service Manager Cookbook*)

Planning and defining compliance reports

The goal of compliance reports is to answer two things: *"How am I doing"* and *"How effectively am I doing it"* especially with regard to helping the business understand current and future threats.

This recipe gives an overview on how to plan compliance reports.

Getting ready

Research the regulatory requirements using your country's respective laws, industry standards, and regulation. This will ensure your reports are relative only to your business and technical compliance objectives. For example, there are standards such as SOX section 404 that demand reports with certain criteria.

How to do it...

There are going to be at least two different types of reports you must plan for:

- ▶ Compliance status or audit reports
- ▶ Stakeholder-targeted reports

Compliance status / audit reports

Compliance status / audit reports are based on your controls. For these reports to answer the question about the actual compliance status and the effectiveness of the compliance program for your business, careful considerations have to be made as to which control activities will produce your business objectives. Therefore, the planning stage of these reports is already completed by the planning of your control objectives and their verification through control activities.

With regard to System Center, out-of-the-box reports will be sufficient for many of these compliance status reports and audit reports. The following table provides some examples of out-of-the-box compliance status information reports, which System Center tool the reports belong to, and the target group:

Category	Out-of-the-box report name in System Center tools	System Center tool	Report target group
Compliance on configuration settings	Summary compliance by the configuration baseline	System Center Configuration Manager	CISO
Compliance on configuration settings	List of assets by compliance state for a configuration baseline	System Center Configuration Manager	Compliance team / IT Security team

Category	Out-of-the-box report name in System Center tools	System Center tool	Report target group
Compliance on configuration settings (drill down report on controls)	Software Update – Compliance 4	System Center Configuration Manager	Person responsible for remediation: Either IT application owner or compliance/IT Security team
Compliance on breach information / policy compliance	Policy_Account Policy Changed	System Center Operations Manager	Compliance team / IT Security team
Compliance on breach information / policy compliance	Audit_Report	System Center Operations Manager	CISO and/or audit team
Compliance on all control/ security breaches and manual controls	Report on the compliance issues category by system security	System Center Service Manager	CISO and compliance team / IT security team

As mentioned in the *Getting ready* section of this recipe, be aware that several laws and industry standards demand certain formats for audit reports. In cases where the System Center out-of-the-box reports do not fulfill them, customized reports will have to be used.

Stakeholder-targeted reports

The purpose of these reports is to keep the stakeholder of your company informed about the compliance program. Therefore, the following questions must be answered:

- Who is the target audience of this report?
- What is your goal for this report?
- What input/output data can provide the required information?
- Who is responsible for the report (owner)?
- What is the frequency of the reports?
- How do you want to present this report?
- What is the improvement process on reports including data source input/output and controls?

We will focus on the first question. You will have to consider reports for different levels such as the following:

- CEO and/or board members
- CISO and/or IT/Security team
- IT application owner

Depending on the targeted audience of the report, different input/output values have to be used and sometimes, translation of inputs/outputs must be used. The following table is an example of possible report considerations:

Target group	Goal	Example report content
IT application owner	Technical compliance status of systems	Exact number of failed/successful controls, including the values For example, number of systems with missing patches/overall system status with drill down of individual systems to include the names of missing patches
CISO and compliance team	Overall compliance standing	Complete compliance reports focusing on threats, vulnerabilities, access management, and policy compliance
CEO/board members	Compliance with regard to business	Focusing on compliance reports translated to business terms that have an impact on areas such as reputation and profit; so translation would be something like promoted, generated, accounted for revenues/growth, or increased/decreased costs/risks

Using out-of-the-box reports from System Center tools will be possible for reports targeting IT application owners, CISO, the IT Security team, or the compliance team. Reports based on the analysis of certain control input/output data will either be accomplished using customized reports within System Center Service Manager or using additional tools such as System Center Orchestrator or dashboards.

Regardless of the actual report, during the planning phase, several principles, that will increase the value of the reports to the business, should be followed. These principals are as follows:

- The overall report should be **complete** for its context
- The input of these reports should be consistently **measured**, at a low cost and preferably, as a number or percentage in context
- The output should be **relevant**
- The input and output should be **transparent**

Complete

Based on previous experience, compliance and IT security staff, while attempting to create reports, put in as much information and statistics as possible. In general, the report must be complete for the context it is designed for. So, on a CISO level, besides technical controls, manual controls including policy or process compliance may have to be included. Still, the report must be concise too.

As a best practice, start out with the out-of-the-box reports provided by the System Center tools as they offer a large number of compliance reports.

Measurable

Being measurable is a key principle for creating valuable reports. The input and output data source or control should be measured in a consistent way. So, two different people using the same control at the same time should produce the same output. As much as possible, control should be automated to ensure this consistency and also to minimize cost. In case the control has to be done manually, it is essential that the people performing them do this in a consistent way. To accomplish this goal, each control should be documented; for example, there should be a document on the IT compliance for identity and access management. For the general users, one important document is the password policy, which should answer the questions why, what, how, and by whom. For IT people, there should be an additional document stating the technical implementation and automated or manual control, to ensure compliance with the password policy. In addition, it should mention how the control activity should be performed.

In addition, whenever possible, controls used for reports should be expressed in numbers or percentage against a unit. For example, a control saying "10 systems out of 100 systems" have missing critical security updates, provides a clear value for a decision on what to do next, compared to a control with the value of "medium".

Relevant

This principle is important especially for the stakeholder-targeted reports. Reports should include controls or output that help the targeted audience in decision making. So the question of to whom the report will be provided is a decision factor on what to include and how to present the report. The IT security staff or compliance team requires the exact numbers of controls, for example, that 10 systems from 100 systems have missing critical security updates, whereas the IT application owner requires a drill down on which systems and security updates were missing.

Transparent

The target audience of a report must understand the controls or output used in the report. The labels should be plain and consistent; and clear measures for controls or input/output should be used. In addition, they must understand how these results came to be. This is especially true for indexes that comprise several controls. If this is the case, it should be clear as to which controls are included. If possible, indexes should be avoided as they average out the value presented in the report; for example, System Center Service Manager allows a report on incidents in the category under **Security Compliance** | **System Security**. The overall status of System Security may be green, as all controls besides the patch management control relating to critical security update did not report any issues. In case the affected systems hold sensitive information or are accessible by the public, this could be a factor in the decision process for immediate remediation steps. Understanding which controls are within the System Security category and being able to drill down into those controls or input/output used is important for a report.

How it works...

The focus is to give you an understanding of the type of reports you should consider and some basic considerations you should include in planning your reports.

The first step is the planning of your control activities. If the control activities do not provide a measure of the effectiveness of your control objectives, then no report will be able to answer this question. Hence, qualified input/output controls are required. In this regard, the stakeholder of controls must provide input and sometimes must be included to improve processes or controls.

Use the questions in this recipe to start out with the creation of your reports, but keep in mind that you have to adapt the information provided here to meet your business requirements and objectives.

There's more...

All System Center reports are based on the SQL Reporting service. This means you can create customized reports should the out-of-the-box reports provide the information you require.

See also

Detailed information on how to plan and implement reports based on System Center may be found in the book *Security Metrics*, *Andrew Jaquith*, *Addison-Wesley Professional* (`http://www.amazon.com/Security-Metrics-Andrew-Jaquith-ebook/dp/B0050G2RC8`).

Security Metrics is a book focusing more on effective measuring of IT security operations. It provides insights into implementing qualitative and meaningful data sources, ensuring reports that provide knowledge to help make the right strategic decisions.

Look out for an upcoming cookbook by Sam Erskine from Packt Publishing. This book on System Center Reporting will provide detailed information on how to plan and implement reports based on System Center.

7

Configuring a Compliance Program in Microsoft System Center 2012 Service Manager

In this chapter, we will cover the following topics:

- ▶ Configuring connectors in System Center 2012 Service Manager to support a compliance program
- ▶ Adding Configuration Items manually in System Center 2012 Service Manager to support a compliance program
- ▶ Configuring compliance process Incident Classification Categories in System Center 2012 Service Manager
- ▶ Adding support groups in System Center 2012 Service Manager to support the compliance program
- ▶ Creating compliance program Incident templates in System Center 2012 Service Manager

Introduction

This chapter provides recipes to configure **Microsoft System Center 2012 Service Manager** (**SCSM 2012**). The configuration of SCSM 2012 will focus on the planning of a compliance program described in *Chapter 6, Planning a Compliance Program in Microsoft System Center 2012*.

After the planning phase of the compliance program in Microsoft System Center 2012 is completed, SCSM 2012 will be configured in this chapter, which covers the following settings and configurations:

- Connecting Active Directory to SCSM 2012
- Connecting Microsoft System Center 2012 Configuration Manager (SCCM 2012) to SCSM 2012
- Connecting Microsoft System Center 2012 Operations Manager (SCOM 2012) to SCSM 2012
- Adding **Configuration Items** (**CIs**) manually in SCSM 2012
- Adding Incident Classification Category list items in SCSM 2012
- Adding Incident Support Group list items in SCSM 2012
- Creating compliance program Incident templates in System Center 2012 Service Manager

The prerequisites for all the following recipes are installed in the Microsoft System Center 2012 Service Manager environment. This includes the following:

- SCSM 2012 Management Server
- SCSM 2012 Data Warehouse Server
- SCSM 2012 Self-Service Portal (optional)

 Detailed information on how to deploy all the System Center 2012 Service Manager components can be found in the Microsoft TechNet library article *Deploying System Center 2012 – Service Manager* (`http://technet.microsoft.com/en-us/library/hh495575.aspx`).

All these recipes should work with System Center 2012 Server Manager, System Center 2012 SP1 Service Manager, and System Center 2012 R2 Service Manager.

Configuring connectors in System Center 2012 Service Manager to support a compliance program

Compliance is related to all kinds of devices and people. To manage compliance in SCSM 2012, it is required to add CIs to the **Configuration Management Database** (**CMDB**) of Microsoft System Center 2012 Service Manager. Most of the required information already exists in other IT components such as Active Directory, System Center 2012 Configuration Manager, and/or System Center 2012 Operations Manager. Connectors in SCSM 2012 can be used to synchronize the information in the CMDB to decrease the work of manually adding these items. Also, the connectors keep changes on these objects in sync with SCSM 2012 (for instance, the phone number of a user or details of newly installed software on a computer).

Getting ready

The following are the prerequisites before you start adding connectors in SCSM 2012:

- A running instance of Active Directory
- A running instance of System Center 2012 Configuration Manager Server
- A running instance of System Center 2012 Operations Manager

 For all connectors, we need an account with appropriate permissions. A detailed list and description can be found in the Microsoft TechNet library article *Accounts Required During Setup* (`http://technet.microsoft.com/en-us/library/hh495662.aspx`).

Before we set up an Operations Manager connector, we must import the base management packs.

Importing Operations Manager 2007 requires the followings steps:

1. Open a PowerShell window with the option **Run as administrator**.
2. Enter the following command:

   `Set-ExecutionPolicy Unrestricted`

3. Select **Yes** and then enter the following commands:

   `Set-Location \"Program Files\Microsoft System Center 2012\Service Manager\Operations Manager Management Packs"`

   `.\installOMMPs.ps1`

4. Close the PowerShell window.

Importing Operations Manager 2012 requires the following steps:

1. Open the Service Manager console and navigate to **Administration | Management Packs**.
2. On the right-hand side, within the task pane under **Management Packs**, click on **Import**.
3. In the **Select Management Packs to Import** window, click on **Add** and navigate to the folder where Service Manager is installed: `Program Files\Microsoft System Center 2012\Service Manager\Operations Manager 2012 Management Packs`.
4. In the **Change the File Type** drop-down menu, select **MP Files (*.mp)**.
5. Choose all the management packs displayed and click on **Open**.
6. In the **Import Management Packs** window, click on **Import**.
7. After the import process is complete, click on **OK**.

Repeat steps 3 to 7 in the folders `Operations Manager 2012` and/or `Operations Manager 2012 SP1` and `Operations Manager 2012 R2`, depending on the version of System Center Operations Manager in your environment.

You have to import all additional management packs of System Center Operations Manager, for instance, Exchange MP, SQL MP, and Operating Systems MPs, in the same way, to get all the classes added in SCSM.

How to do it...

The next sections guide you through the configuration of all three connectors.

Configuring the Active Directory connector

Perform the following steps to configure the Active Directory connector:

1. Open the Service Manager console and navigate to **Administration | Connectors**.

2. On the right-hand side within the task pane, click on **Create Connector** and select **Active Directory connector**.

3. In the **Active Directory connector wizard**, within the **Before You Begin** page, click on **Next**.

4. Enter a name for this connector in the **Name** field of the **General** page. We will use `AD Connector` in our recipe as the name.

5. Add a description in the **Description** field. This is optional.

6. Make sure the option **Enable this connector** is checked:

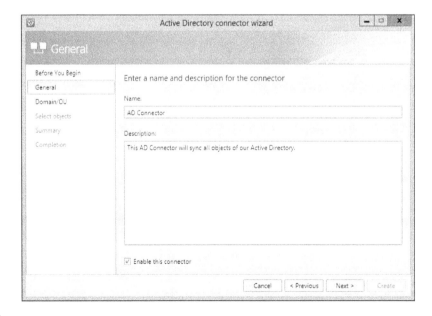

7. Click on **Next**.

8. On the **Domain or Organizational Unit** page of the **Active Directory connector wizard**, we will specify **Server Information | Use the domain: <your domain>**. In our example it is hudcloud.de.

9. Add a new Run As account with the appropriate permissions for this connector by clicking on **New** in the **Credentials** section.

10. Fill in the required information in the **Run As Account** page:

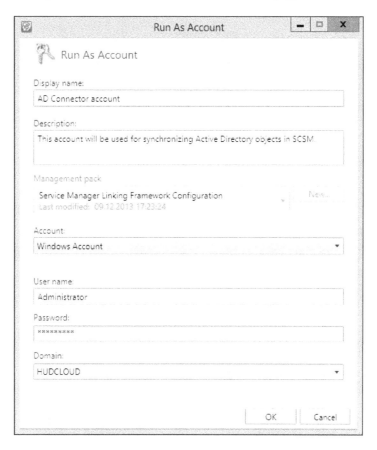

11. Click on **OK** in the **Run As Account** page.

12. Click on **Next** in the **Active Directory connector wizard** page.

13. On the **Select objects** page, select **All computers, printers, users and user groups**.

14. Select **Automatically add users of AD Groups imported by this connector** as well as **Do not write null values for properties that are not set in Active Directory** as shown in the following screenshot:

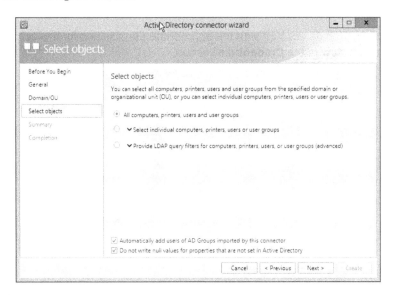

15. Click on **Next**.

16. Check the **Summary** page and click on **Create**:

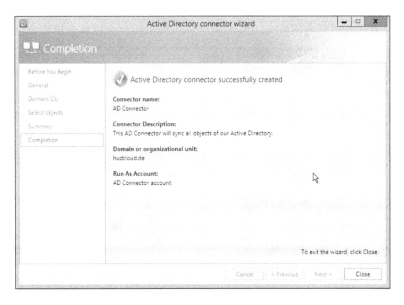

17. Click on **Close** on the **Completion** page.

Configuring the Configuration Manager Connector

Perform the following steps to configure the Configuration Manager Connector:

1. Open the Service Manager console and navigate to **Administration** | **Connectors**.

2. Within the task pane on the right-hand side, choose **Create Connector** and select **Configuration Manager Connector**.

3. In the **System Center Configuration Manager connector wizard** window within the **Before You Begin** page, click on **Next**.

4. Enter a name for this connector in the **Name** field of the **General** page. We will use SCCM Connector in our recipe as the name.

5. Add a description in the **Description** field. This is optional.

6. Make sure the **Enable** option is selected:

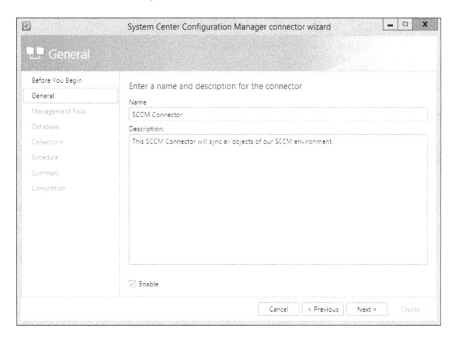

7. Click on **Next**.

8. On the **Management Pack** page, select **System Center Configuration Manager 2012 Connector Configuration** (or **System Center Configuration Manager Connector Configuration** if you run a System Center Configuration Manager 2007 infrastructure).

9. Click on **Next**.

10. On the **Database** page, specify the **Database server name** and the **Database** name.

11. Add a new Run As account with the appropriate permissions for this connector by clicking on **New** in the **Credentials** section.

12. Fill in the required information in the **Run As Account** page:

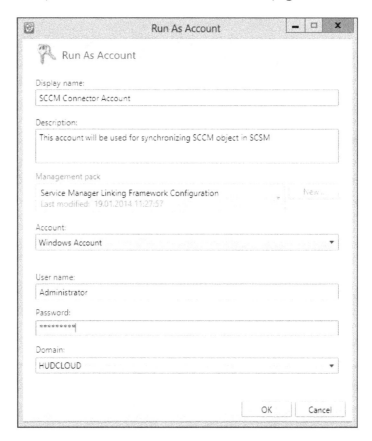

13. Click on the **OK** button.

14. In the **Database** page of the wizard, click on **Next**.

15. On the **Collections** page of the **System Center Configuration Manager connector wizard**, select the **Select all** as well as **Do not write null values for properties that are not set in Configuration Manager** options:

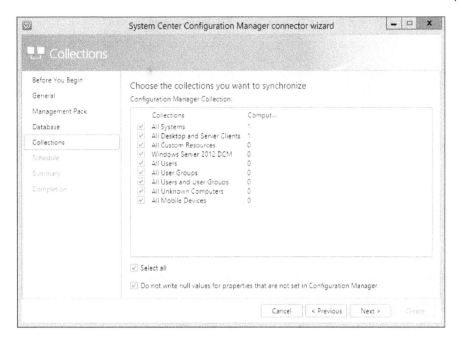

16. Click on **Next**.

17. On the **Schedule** page of the wizard, choose the **Every day** value as **3:00** in the **Create a schedule** section.

18. Click on **Next**.

19. Verify the information on the **Summary** page and click on **Create**:

20. Click on **Close** on the **Completion** page.

Configuring Operations Manager CI connector

Perform the following steps to configure the Operations Manager CI connector:

1. Open the Service Manager console and navigate to **Administration | Connectors**.

2. On the right-hand side within the task pane, choose **Create Connector** and select **Operations Manager CI connector**.

3. In the **Operations Manager CI connector wizard** window, within the **Before You Begin** page, click on **Next**.

4. Enter a name for this connector in the **Name** field of the **General** page. We will use `Ops Manager CI Connector` in our recipe as the name.

5. Add a description in the **Description** field. This is optional.

6. Make sure the **Enable** option is selected.

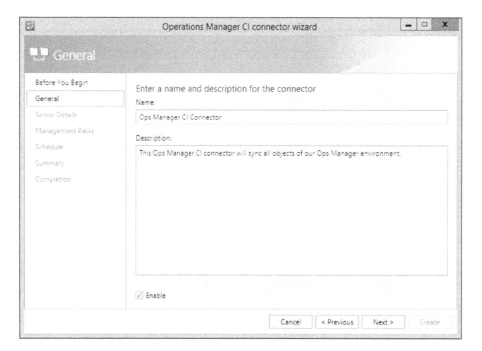

7. Click on the **Next** button.

8. In the **Server Details** page, specify your Operations Manager Server in the **Server name** section.

9. Add a new Run As account with the appropriate permissions for this connector by clicking on **New** in the **Credentials** section.

10. Fill in the required information in the **Run As Account** page:

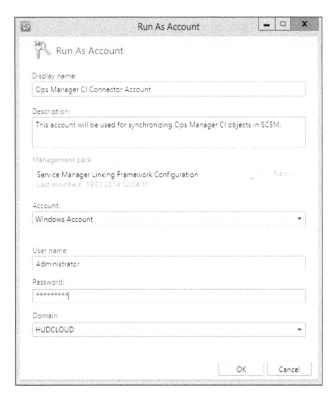

11. Click on **OK**.

12. Click on **Next** on the **Server Details** page of the wizard.

13. On the **Management Packs** page in the wizard, mark **Select all** as well as **Do not write null values for properties that are not set in Operations Manager**.

14. Click on **Next**.

15. On the **Schedule** page of the wizard, choose the **Every day** value as **4:AM<** in the **Create a schedule** section.

16. Click on **Next**.

17. Verify the information on the **Summary** page of the wizard and click on **Create**:

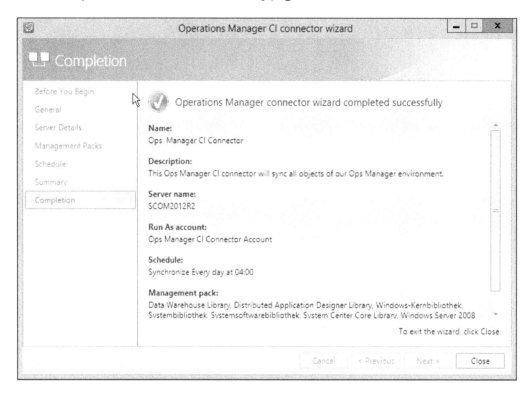

18. On the **Completion** page of the wizard, click on **Close**.

How it works...

After each connector in SCSM 2012 is configured properly, the data will be synced from the source system to the CMDB of SCSM 2012 automatically.

This synchronization is based on a schedule, defined in the SCCM and Ops Manager connector, or an interval. The AD Connector will run every 24 hours.

All synchronized objects in the CMDB of SCSM 2012 can be modified in SCSM manually. If there is a conflict, for example, if the phone number of a user is set to 123 in AD and is manually modified in SCSM to 456, the connector will overwrite the phone number during the next synchronization. The activated option, **Do not write null values for properties that are not set in xyz**, prevents the attribute from being overwritten if it's not set in the source system but manually added in SCSM.

There's more...

It is possible to create more than one connector in SCSM to synchronize data from additional systems.

Adding more than one connector in SCSM

It's possible to add more than one AD, SCCM, or Ops Manager Connector in SCSM 2012. This may be needed for complex and distributed IT infrastructures. The configuration steps are the same as those for the first connector.

See also

▶ `http://technet.microsoft.com/en-us/library/hh524326.aspx` (Microsoft TechNet library article *Using Connectors to Import Data into System Center 2012 – Service Manager*)

▶ `http://www.packtpub.com/microsoft-system-center-service-manager-2012-cookbook/book` (refer to *Chapter 4* of *Microsoft System Center 2012 Service Manager Cookbook*)

▶ `http://blogs.technet.com/b/thomase/archive/2013/04/08/scsm-active-directory-connector-optimization.aspx` (the *SCSM Active Directory Connector optimization* article on TechNet Blogs)

Adding Configuration Items manually in System Center 2012 Service Manager to support a compliance program

If an object you need in the compliance program (for example, CI) isn't available in one of the source systems (Active Directory, System Center 2012 Configuration Manager, or System Center 2012 Operations Manager), you can add CIs manually in System Center 2012 Service Manager. This recipe will explain how to add a user manually. The same process can also be used to add a computer as a CI.

Getting ready

In *Chapter 6, Planning a Compliance Program in Microsoft System Center 2012*, we planned and defined the responsibilities for the compliance program. It could be the case that a responsible person doesn't exist in the Active Directory, for instance, an external person without an account in AD. Thus, a responsible and defined person should be documented and added manually in SCSM 2012.

We have to verify that the user we need for our compliance program in SCSM 2012 does not already exist. Perform the following steps to do so:

1. In the SCSM console, navigate to **Configuration Items | Users**.

2. Type the first and last name of the person in the **Filter** section. For instance, `Peter Auditor`.

If there are no matches found, the user does not exist in the CMDB of SCSM 2012.

How to do it...

To add a user manually in the SCSM 2012 CMDB, perform the following steps:

1. In the SCSM console, navigate to **Configuration Items | Users**.

2. In the **Tasks** pane on the right-hand side of the SCSM console, click on **Create User**.

3. Fill in all the information you need in the **User** form and click on **OK**:

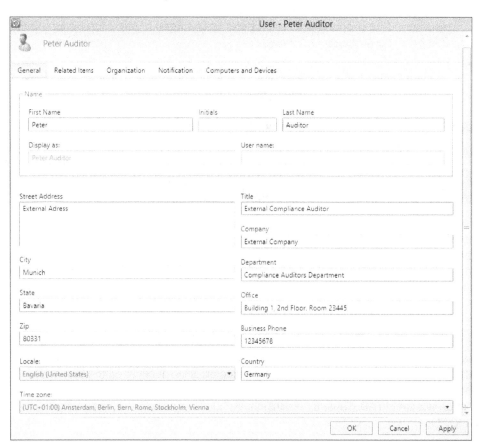

4. Click on the **Notification** tab in the **User** form.

5. To add an e-mail address for this user, click on **Add** next to the **Notification addresses** section.

6. Fill in the information in the **User Notification** form:

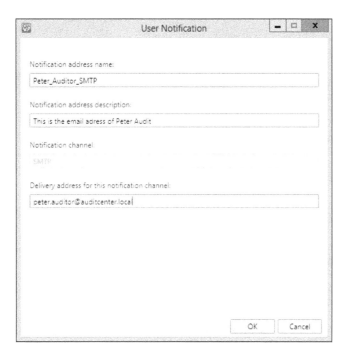

7. Click on **OK**.

8. In the **User** form, click on **OK**.

How it works...

Each Configuration Item in SCSM 2012 CMDB can be used in every IT management process as a Related Item. The relationships could be as follows:

▶   Persons/users can be **Affected User** or **Assigned to User** of a compliance-program-related Incident in SCSM 2012. Also, users/persons can be notified automatically by e-mail if an e-mail address is available for this CI.

▶   A computer can be an Affected Item of a compliance-program-related Incident or Change Request.

Perform the following steps to verify that the user has been added in SCSM successfully:

1. In the SCSM console, navigate to **Configuration Items | Users** or refresh the **Users** list in the SCSM console.

2. Type the first and last name of the person in the **Filter** section. For instance, `Peter Auditor`.

   The user should be found, as shown in the following screenshot :

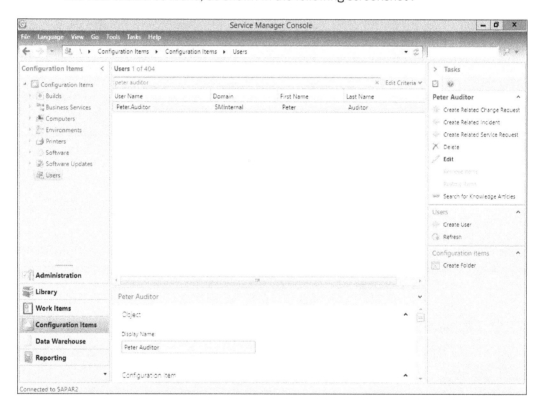

There's more...

It is possible to import Configuration Items manually in the CMDB. Also, you can add missing classes of CIs in SCSM 2012.

Importing CIs manually via CSV

It may happen that a large number of CIs need to be added in the SCSM CMDB because they do not exist in any system but are required for the compliance process. SCSM 2012 offers an import of CIs using a CSV file. This topic is covered in *Chapter 4* of the book *Microsoft System Center 2012 Service Manager Cookbook, Packt Publishing*.

Adding new classes in SCSM 2012

If a required class for the compliance program does not exist in SCSM 2012 by default, and it isn't available as a management pack of Microsoft System Center Operations Manager, it is possible to create a custom Configuration Item class. Detailed information how to do this can be found in the following:

- ▶ *Chapter 10* of *Microsoft System Center 2012 Service Manager Cookbook*, *Packt Publishing* (`http://www.packtpub.com/microsoft-system-center-service-manager-2012-cookbook/book`)

- ▶ The *System Center: Service Manager Engineering Blog: Creating Custom Configuration Item Classes Using the Service Manager Authoring Tool* article at `http://blogs.technet.com/b/servicemanager/archive/2010/09/29/creating-custom-configuration-item-classes-using-the-service-manager-authoring-tool.aspx`

See also

- ▶ `http://technet.microsoft.com/en-us/library/hh519814.aspx` (the Microsoft TechNet library article *Using a CSV File to Import Data into Service Manager*)

- ▶ `http://technet.microsoft.com/en-us/library/ff460987.aspx` (the TechNet library article *Configuration Items in Service Manager*)

- ▶ `http://www.packtpub.com/microsoft-system-center-service-manager-2012-cookbook/book` (*Chapter 4* of *Microsoft System Center 2012 Service Manager Cookbook*)

Configuring compliance process Incident Classification Categories in System Center 2012 Service Manager

Incident Classification Categories in System Center 2012 Service Manager are helpful to route Incidents to the related support group. Also , the Incident Classification Categories can be used in reporting to monitor **Key Performance Indicators** (**KPIs**) and for auditing compliance. This recipe will explain how to add additional Incident Classification Categories to support the compliance management process.

Getting ready

The *Planning System Center Service Manager 2012 related settings and configuration* recipe of *Chapter 6*, *Planning a Compliance Program in Microsoft System Center 2012*, should be completed and documented before you begin with this recipe.

We will work with the planned Incident Classification Categories defined in *Chapter 6,
Planning a Compliance Program in Microsoft System Center 2012*:

Category (top level)	Category (first child level)	Use of category
Compliance Issue	This is the root level of the Classification Categories list	Generic Incident Classification Category
Compliance Issue	System Security	All compliance issues that are related to System Security; for instance, password policy and access policy
Compliance Issue	Facility	All compliance issues that are related to facility objects; for instance, access control of data centers
Compliance Issue	Perimeter Security	All compliance issues that are related to network security; for instance, network encryption, firewalls, and network intrusion detection
Compliance Issue	Data Privacy	All compliance issues that are related to data privacy; for instance, unauthorized data access

How to do it...

To add the compliance program **Incident Classification Categories**, navigate in SCSM
console to **Library | Lists** and perform the following steps:

1. In the **Lists** pane, filter for **Incident Classification**.

2. Open the **Incident Classification** list by double-clicking on the name.

3. Click on **Add Item** on the right-hand side of the form. A new list item will be added at
   the end of the list.

4. Select the **List Value** item we added and change the name of the list value to
    Compliance Issue. Add a description (optional).

5. With **Compliance Issue** still selected, click on **Add Child**.

6. Select the new added child list item and rename it to `System Security`.
    Add a description (optional):

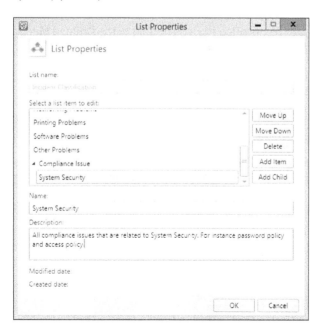

7. Repeat steps 5 and 6 until all compliance-programs-related Incident Classification categories defined in the previous table are added.

8. Click on **OK** in the **List Properties** form.

How it works...

In the compliance program process, Incident Classification can be used for the following compliance-program-related tasks:

▶ Routing of compliance-related Incidents to the related and responsible Support Group in SCSM

▶ Determining the appropriated priority of a compliance issue in SCSM, based on the urgency and impact of a compliance issue category

▶ Getting reports and KPIs for specific compliance program issues

▶ Supporting the compliance audit with reports based on different types of compliance categories

There's more...

Categories for the Change Management process can be added and related to the compliance program as well.

Adding compliance-program-related categories for Change Management

If you have planned your compliance process related to the Change Management process, you can introduce additional **Change Areas** in SCSM 2012 as well.

To add the compliance program **Change Area**, navigate in the SCSM console to **Library | Lists** and perform the following steps:

1. In the **Lists** pane, filter for `Change Area`.

2. Open the **Change Area** list by double-clicking on the name.

3. Click on **Add Item** on the right-hand side of the form. A new list item will be added at the end of the list.

4. Select the **List Value** item we added and change the name of the list value to
    Compliance. Add a description (optional):

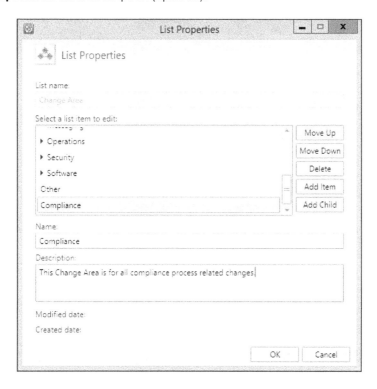

5. Add all child list items in the **Change Area** list as planned, defined, and documented
    in _Chapter 6, Planning a Compliance Program in Microsoft System Center 2012_.

6. Click on **OK** in the **List Properties** form.

See also

▶ `http://technet.microsoft.com/en-us/library/hh495620.aspx` (the
    TechNet library article _Using Groups, Queues, and Lists in System Center 2012 –
    Service Manager_)

▶ `http://www.packtpub.com/microsoft-system-center-service-
    manager-2012-cookbook/book` (_Chapter 6_ of _Microsoft System Center 2012
    Service Manager Cookbook_)

Adding support groups in System Center 2012 Service Manager to support the compliance program

In a compliance program, different groups could be responsible for different compliance issues. Details should be planned, defined, and documented. (Refer to *Chapter 6, Planning a Compliance Program in Microsoft System Center 2012*).

Getting ready

In this recipe, we will configure Support Groups in SCSM 2012 based on the following table, which is the result of the compliance program planning phase:

Compliance Category (top level)	Compliance Category (first child level)	Responsible support group
Compliance Issue	This is the root level of the Classification Categories list	Tier 1
Compliance Issue	System Security	AD and Server Admin Support Group
Compliance Issue	Facility	IT Facility Management
Compliance Issue	Perimeter Security	Network and Perimeter Admin Support Group
Compliance Issue	Data Privacy	Data Privacy Officer Support Group

How to do it...

Perform the following steps to create the needed Support Groups in SCSM 2012:

1. Navigate in the SCSM console to **Library | Lists**.
2. In the **Lists** pane, filter for **Incident Tier Queue**.
3. Open the **Incident Classification** list by double-clicking on the name.
4. Click on **Add Item** on the right-hand side of the form. A new list item will be added at the end of the list.
5. Select the **List Value** item we added and change the name of the list value to **AD** and **Server Admin Support Group**. Add a description (optional).

6. Repeat steps 4 and 5 for **IT Facility Management**, **Network and Perimeter Admin Support Group**, and **Data Privacy Officer Support Group**.

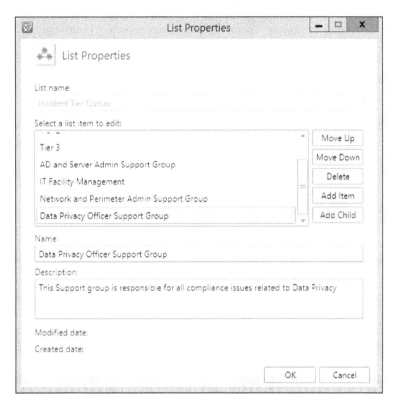

7. Click on **OK** in the **List Properties** form.

How it works...

Support groups in SCSM 2012 help in routing compliance-related Incidents to the responsible teams or people. They also act as a filter for Incidents that can be created in SCSM 2012 based on the support group.

There's more...

Additional views can be created in SCSM 2012 based on the newly-created support groups.

Creating a new view for compliance-related Incidents based on the support group in SCSM 212

To get a fast overview of all compliance-related Incidents, it's very helpful to create different views based on different attributes. These attributes can be in any combination:

- Incident Classification (compliance-program-related Incident Classification)
- Support group (compliance-program-related support groups)
- Status of the Incident (Active, Pending, Resolved, or Closed)

How to get started with creating your own custom views is described in the TechNet Library article *Create a New View* (`http://technet.microsoft.com/en-us/library/hh519588.aspx`).

See also

- `http://blogs.technet.com/b/antoni/archive/2012/08/13/service-manager-101-part-1-incident-management.aspx` (the *Service Manager 101 – Focus on Incident Management* article on TechNet Blogs)
- `http://technet.microsoft.com/en-us/library/hh495524.aspx` (the *How to Customize a View* article on TechNet library)
- `http://www.packtpub.com/microsoft-system-center-service-manager-2012-cookbook/book` (*Chapter 2* of *Microsoft System Center 2012 Service Manager Cookbook*)

Creating compliance program Incident templates in System Center 2012 Service Manager

Incident templates in SCSM 2012 are prefilled Incident forms. These may include a predefined Title, Description, Urgency, Impact, and Support Group or Assigned User in the Incident record.

Templates offer a consistency for all newly created Incidents in the compliance process.

Getting ready

Before we start creating Incident templates, you should finish all previous recipes within this chapter:

- *Configuring connectors in System Center 2012 Service Manager to support a compliance program*
- *Adding Configuration Items manually in System Center 2012 Service Manager to support a compliance program*

- ▸ *Configuring compliance process Incident Classification Categories in System Center 2012 Service Manager*

- ▸ *Adding Support Groups in System Center 2012 Service Manager to support the compliance program*

Also, the priority calculation in the **Incident Settings** window of SCSM should be done. You can verify this by navigating to **Administration | Incident Settings** in the SCSM console, as shown in the following screenshot:

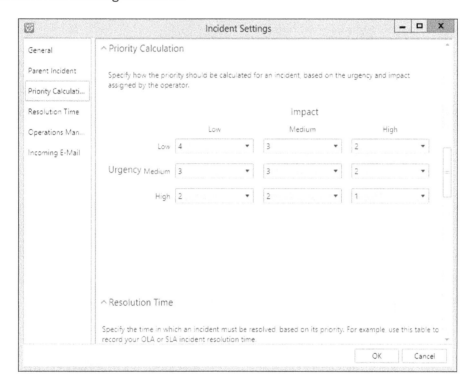

How to do it...

To create compliance program Incident templates, perform the following steps:

1. Navigate in the SCSM console to **Library | Templates**.

2. Go to the **Tasks** pane on the right-hand side of the SCSM console and click on **Create Template**.

3. Enter a name and a description (optional) in the fields **Name** and **Description**. In our example, we will use `Compliance Issue Incident Template` as the name of the Incident template.

4. In the **Class** section, click on **Browse ....**.

5. Select **Incident** and click on **OK** in the **Select a Class** form.

6. Click on **New...** in the **Management Pack** section.

7. Specify a name and a description for the management pack:

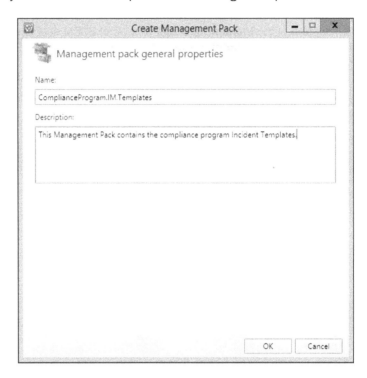

8. Click **OK** in the **Create Management Pack** form.

9. Click **OK** in the **Create Template** form.

10. In the **Incident Template** form, specify all information in the fields we have defined in *Chapter 6, Planning a Compliance Program in Microsoft System Center 2012*, and configured in the recipes of this chapter:

11. Click on **OK** in the **Incident Template – Compliance Issue Incident Template** form.

12. Repeat steps 2 through 11 for all Incident templates that we need for all defined Incident Classification categories.

> All compliance program Incident templates should be stored in the same Management Pack.

How it works...

A prepopulated template can be used to create a new compliance-program-related Incident Record in SCSM 2012. By using templates, the required and optional information of an Incident Record form is kept consistent. In addition, time is saved during the creation process.

Consistency of data can be very important in a compliance program during the audit phase.

There's more...

It is possible to add Change Request templates in SCSM 2012 as well.

Adding compliance program Change Request templates in SCSM 2012

Perform the following steps to create compliance-program-related Change Request templates:

1. Navigate in the SCSM console to **Library | Templates**.

2. In the **Tasks** pane on the right-hand side of the SCSM console, click on **Create Template**.

3. Enter a name and a description (optional) in the fields **Name** and **Description** respectively. In our example, we will use `Compliance Issue Change Request Template` as the name of the Change Request template.

4. In the **Class** section, click on **Browse ...**.

5. Select **Change Request** and click on **OK** in the **Select a Class** form.

6. Click on **New...** in the **Management Pack** section.

7. Specify a name and a description for the Management Pack; for instance, `ComplianceProgram.CM.Templates`, and click on **OK**.

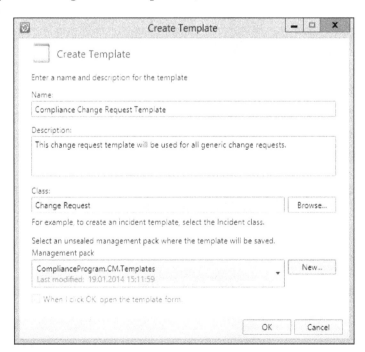

8. Click on **OK** in the **Create Template** form.

9. In the **Change Request Template** form, specify all information in the fields we have defined in *Chapter 6, Planning a Compliance Program in Microsoft System Center 2012,* and configured in the recipes of this chapter.

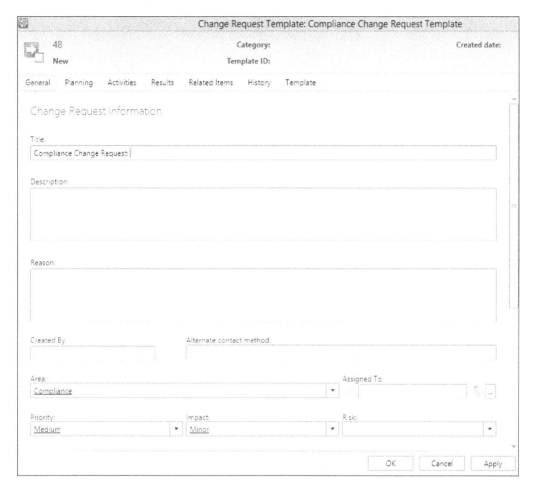

10. Click on **OK** in the **Change Request Template: Compliance Change Request Template** form.

11. Repeat steps 2 to 10 for all Change Request templates we need for all defined Change Request areas.

 All compliance program Change Request templates should be stored in the same Management Pack.

See also

▸ http://technet.microsoft.com/en-us/library/hh495580.aspx
(TechNet library article *How to Customize a Template*)

▸ http://technet.microsoft.com/en-us/library/hh495665.aspx
(TechNet library article *How to Create Incident Templates*)

▸ http://technet.microsoft.com/en-us/library/ff460883.aspx
(TechNet library article *How to Create Change Request Templates*)

▸ http://www.packtpub.com/microsoft-system-center-service-
manager-2012-cookbook/book (*Chapter* 6 and *Chapter* 7 of *Microsoft
System Center 2012 Service Manager Cookbook*)

8
Automating Compliance Processes with Microsoft System Center 2012

In this chapter, we will cover the following topics:

- ▶ Planning the automation of the compliance management process
- ▶ Configuring compliance program notifications in Microsoft System Center 2012 Service Manager
- ▶ Forwarding compliance program related alerts
- ▶ Forwarding compliance program related Compliance Settings Management issues

Introduction

Automating the compliance management processes provides consistency and prevents steps from being missed or forgotten.

Also, human errors such as mistyped or inconsistent information can be avoided through process automation.

The prerequisites for all the recipes in this chapter are as follows:

- An installed Microsoft System Center 2012 Service Manager environment. This includes:
    - SCSM 2012 Management Server
    - SCSM 2012 Data Warehouse Server
    - SCSM 2012 Self-Service Portal (optional)

- An installed Microsoft System Center 2012 Operations Manager environment. This includes:
    - SCOM 2012 Management Server

- An installed Microsoft System Center 2012 Configuration Manager environment. This includes:
    - SCCM 2012 Primary Site Server

- The following recipes and chapters also must be read:
    - *Chapter 3, Enhancing the Basic Compliance Program Using Microsoft System Center 2012 Configuration Manager*
    - The *Adding a compliance program monitor in Microsoft System Center 2012 Operations Manager* recipe of *Chapter 4, Monitoring the Basic Compliance Program*
    - The recipes *Configuring compliance process Incident Classification Categories in System Center 2012 Service Manager* and *Creating compliance program Incident templates in System Center 2012 Service Manager* of *Chapter 7, Configuring a Compliance Program in Microsoft System Center 2012 Service Manager*

 All of the recipes should work with System Center 2012 Service Manager, System Center 2012 SP1 Service Manager, and System Center 2012 R2 Service Manager. It's recommended to use the same version of all Microsoft System Center products in the environment.

Planning the automation of the compliance management process

The planning phase is essential to the automation of the compliance management process. In this recipe, we will talk about all the planning steps recommended for the recipes that follow.

Getting ready

The prerequisite for this recipe is a basic knowledge and understanding of the Incident Management process in the organization. This covers the following details as well:

- ▶ Classification of Incidents
- ▶ Prioritization of Incidents using the impact and urgency of the compliance issue

How to do it...

The planning steps for the recipe *Configuring compliance program notification in Microsoft System Center 2012 Service Manager* are as follows:

1. Defining the recipients for notifications on compliance-related incidents:

    1. Define who is responsible for compliance issues and who should be informed on compliance-related issues by e-mail.

    2. In this recipe, the user Peter Ciso should be notified about any compliance-related issue.

    3. Verify that Peter Ciso is an existing user in the SCSM 2012 **Configuration Management Database** (**CMDB**) and that Peter's e-mail address is available in CMDB.

    4. Document the result of this planning step.

2. Defining the compliance-related incidents that need a notification to be sent:

    1. A notification should be sent to the user Peter Ciso for any compliance-related issue.

    2. Document the result of this planning step.

3. Defining the notification text that should be sent for compliance-related incidents.

    The text of the notification e-mail should be as follows:

```
Dear Peter,
A compliance related incident is logged in System Center Server
Manager.
Incident ID: <ID of Incident>
Title: <Title of Incidents>
Description: <Description text of Incident>
Please check the incident.
--- This email was sent by System Center Service Manager ---
```

For the recipe, *Forwarding of compliance program related alerts*, the planning steps are as follows:

1. Defining which compliance-related alerts in SCOM 2012 a corresponding incident in SCSM should be created for:

    1. All alerts defined and configured in the *Adding a compliance program monitor in Microsoft System Center 2012 Operations Manager* recipe of *Chapter 4, Monitoring the Basic Compliance Program*, should be forwarded from SCOM 2012 to SCSM 2012 automatically.

    2. Document the defined alerts to be forwarded and the SCOM 2012 management pack that the SCOM 2012 is stored in. In our recipe, we have used the name `Compliance program failed logon events` for the management pack.

    3. Alerts in SCOM 2012 should be closed if the corresponding Incident in SCSM 2012 is resolved or closed.

    4. Document the result of this planning step.

2. Defining the used Incident Classifications and Incident templates which should be used in SCSM 2012.

    1. For automatically created compliance-related incidents, we will use the SCSM 2012 Incident template we created in *Chapter 7, Configuring a Compliance Program in Microsoft System Center 2012 Service Manager*, in the recipe *Creating compliance program Incident templates in System Center 2012 Service Manager*. This template contains the Incident Classification Categories configured in the recipe *Configuring compliance process Incident Classification Categories in System Center 2012 Service Manager* in *Chapter 7, Configuring a Compliance Program in Microsoft System Center 2012 Service Manager*.

    2. Document the result of this planning step.

For the recipe, *Forwarding compliance program related Compliance Settings Management issues*, the planning steps are as follows:

1. Defining which compliance-related breached baselines in SCCM 2012 a corresponding incident in SCSM should be created for:

    1. For all Compliance Settings Management issues in SCCM 2012, which were defined and configured in *Chapter 3, Enhancing the Basic Compliance Program Using Microsoft System Center 2012 Configuration Manager*, in the recipes *Creating a baseline to monitor unapproved software* and *Creating a baseline to monitor unauthorized hardware and virtual systems*, a corresponding Incident should be created in SCSM 2012 automatically.

    2. Document the result of this planning step.

2. Defining the used Incident Classifications and Incident templates that should be used in SCSM 2012.

   1. For the automatically created compliance-related incidents, we will use the SCSM 2012 Incident template, which we created in *Chapter 7, Configuring a Compliance Program in Microsoft System Center 2012 Service Manager* in the recipe, *Creating compliance program Incident templates in System Center 2012 Service Manager*. This template contains the Incident Classification Categories configured in *Chapter 7, Configuring a Compliance Program in Microsoft System Center 2012 Service Manager* in the recipe, *Configuring compliance process Incident Classification Categories in System Center 2012 Service Manager*.

   2. Document the result of this planning step.

How it works...

In this recipe, all of the details required for the next recipes are defined and documented:

- Defining the recipients of the notification on compliance-related incidents.

- Defining which compliance-related incidents a notification should be sent for

- Defining which compliance-related alerts in SCOM 2012 a corresponding incident in SCSM should be created for

- Defining the used Incident Classifications and Incident templates that should be used in SCSM 2012

- Defining which compliance-related breached baselines in SCCM 2012 a corresponding incident in SCSM should be created for

- Defining the used Incident Classifications

These details will be used to configure the automation processes in each of the following recipes.

Configuring compliance program notification in Microsoft System Center 2012 Service Manager

In this recipe, we will configure e-mail notifications for the people responsible for the compliance program. This offers a consistent and fast way to inform the concerned person or group regarding compliance-program-related issues logged in SCSM 2012.

Getting ready

The following steps need to be completed before starting this recipe:

- Complete the planning recipe in this chapter.

- The user or group that should be notified needs to be created in CDMB in SCSM 2012. This is described in *Chapter 7, Configuring a Compliance Program in Microsoft System Center 2012 Service Manager,* in the recipe, *Configuring connectors in System Center 2012 Service Manager to support a compliance program* and *Adding Configuration Items manually in System Center 2012 Service Manager to support a compliance program.*

- The user or group that should be notified by e-mail needs to have a valid e-mail address configured in SCSM 2012.

- The Operations Manager Connector needs to be configured. This is described in *Chapter 7, Configuring a Compliance Program in Microsoft System Center 2012 Service Manager* in the recipe, *Configuring connectors in System Center 2012 Service Manager to support a compliance program.*

- The Incident Classification categories in SCSM 2012 need to be created as described in *Chapter 7, Configuring a Compliance Program in Microsoft System Center 2012 Service Manager* in the recipe, *Configuring compliance process Incident Classification Categories in System Center 2012 Service Manager.*

- The notification channel in SCSM 2012 needs to be configured with the corresponding settings.

How to do it...

Perform the steps given in the following sections to configure the notification in SCSM 2012.

Creating a notification template for compliance issue notification e-mails

Perform the following steps to create a notification template:

1. Open the SCSM 2012 console and navigate to **Administration** | **Notifications** | **Templates**:

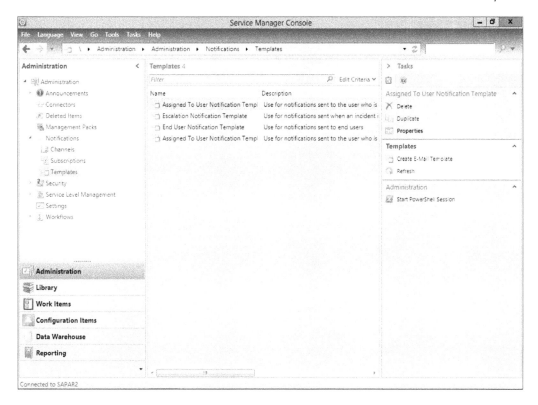

2. Click on **Create E-Mail Templates** in the **Tasks** bar on the right-hand side.

3. Provide a name in the **Notification template name** field. We will use `Notification Template Compliance Issue` in this recipe.

4. Click on **Browse** next to the **Targeted Class** field and choose **Incident** from the list:

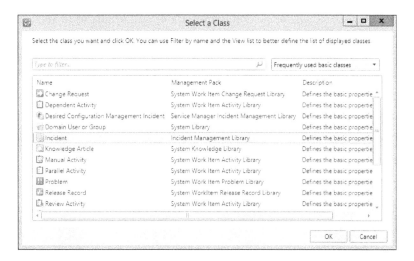

5. Click on **OK**.

6. Click on **New** next to the **Management Pack** field and enter `ComplianceProgram.IM.Notification` in the **Name** field.

7. Enter `This management pack contains the configuration of Compliance Management notification.` in the **Description** field:

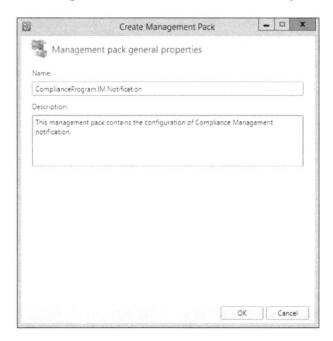

8. Click on **OK**.

9. In the **Create E-Mail Notification Template** form, click on **Next**.

10. In the **Template Design** section of the **Create E-Mail Notification Template** form, check **Send as HTML**.

11. Type `A Compliance Issue Incident is created: []` in the **Message subject** field.

12. Enter the following text in the **Message body** field:

```
Dear Peter,<br>
A compliance related incident is logged in System Center Server
Manager.<br>
Incident ID: []<br>
Title: <br>
Description: <br>
Please check the incident.<br>
--- This email was sent by System Center Service Manager ---
```

13. Click between **[** and **]** in the **Message subject** field.

14. Click on the **Insert** button above the **Message subject** field.

15. Select **ID** in the column on the right-hand side under the **Work Item** section in the **Select Property** form:

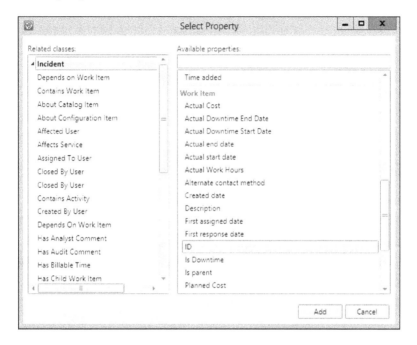

16. Click on **Add**.

17. Click between **[** and **]** in the **Body** field in the **Incident ID: []
** line.

18. Click on the **Insert** button above the **Message subject** field.

19. Select **ID** in the column on the right-hand side under the **Work Item** section in the **Select Property** form.

20. Click on **Add**.

21. Click in front of the **
** tag in the **Title:
** line in the **Message body** field.

22. Click on the **Insert** button above the **Message subject** field.

23. Select **Title** in the column on the right-hand side under the **Work Item** section in the **Select Property** form:

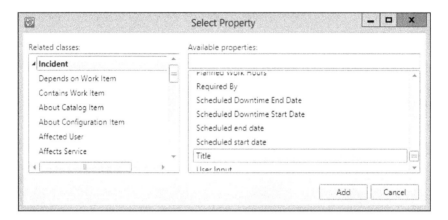

24. Click on **Add**.

25. Click in front of the **
** tag in the **Title:
** line in the **Message body** field.

26. Click on the **Insert** button above the **Message subject** field.

27. Select **Description** in the column on the right-hand side under the **Work Item** section in the **Select Property** form .

28. Click on **Add**. The result should look like the following screenshot:

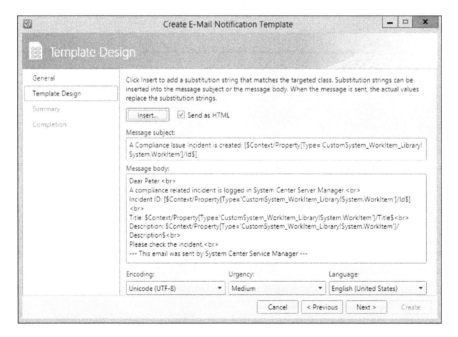

29. Click on **Next**.

30. Verify the summary in the **Create E-Mail Template** form and click on **Create**.

31. Click on **Close**.

32. Verify that the newly created **Notification** template is listed in the SCSM 2012 console:

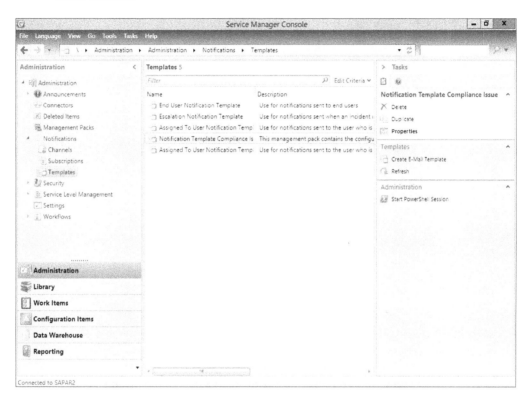

Creating a subscription for compliance issue notification e-mails

Perform the following steps to create a subscription:

1. Navigate to **Administration | Notifications | Subscription**.

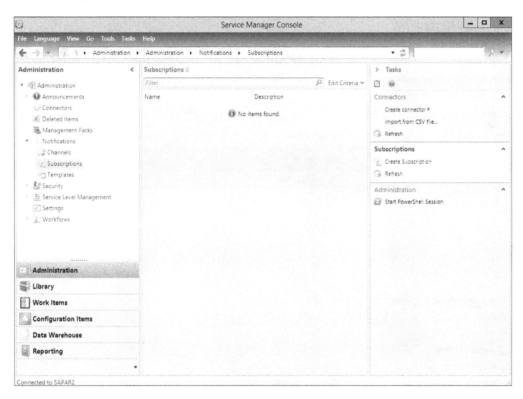

2. Click on **Create Subscription** in the **Tasks** bar on the right-hand side.

3. In the **Create E-Mail Notification Subscription** form, click on **Next**.

4. Enter Notification Workflow On All New Compliance Related Incidents in the **Notification subscription name** field.

5. Enter This notification workflow will send an e-mail for any new created compliance related incident in the **Description (optional)** field.

6. Select the **When an object of the selected class is created** setting in the **When to notify** field.

7. Click on **Browse...** at the **Targeted class** field.

8. Select **Incident** in the list in the **Select a Class** form:

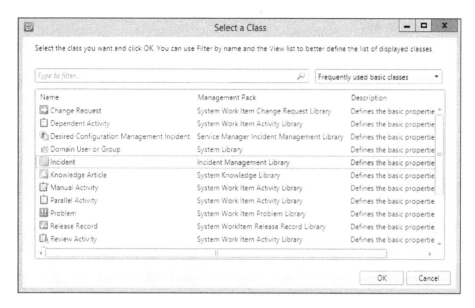

9. Click on **OK**.

10. Select **ComplianceProgram.IM.Notification** in the **Management Pack** field:

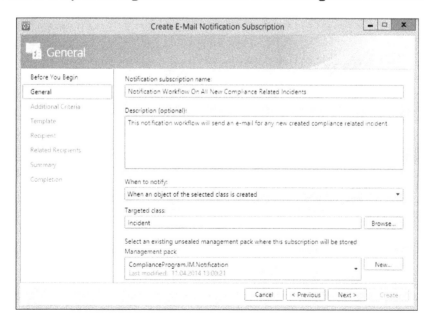

11. Click on **Next**.

12. In the **Additional Criteria** section of the **Create E-Mail Notification Subscription** form, select a value for **Classification category** from the list on the right-hand side and click on **Add**.

13. Repeat step 12 four times to add the **Incident Classification category** five times in the **Criteria** list.

14. In the **Criteria** list, select **Compliance Issue** in the first line as the **equals** criteria.

15. Repeat step 14 for every subclassification category below **Compliance Issue**.

16. The result should look like the following screenshot:

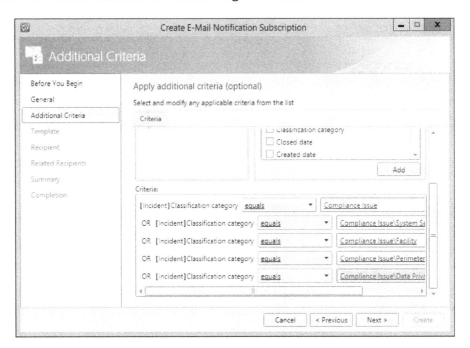

17. Click on **Next**.

18. In the **Template** section of the **Create E-Mail Notification Subscription** form, click on **Select…**.

19. Select **Notification Template Compliance Issue** from the list in the **Select E-Mail Notification Template** form:

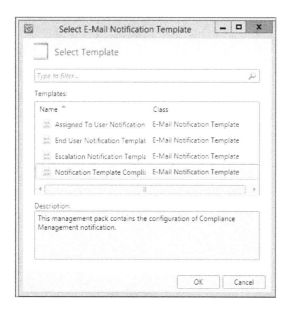

20. Click on **OK**.

21. Click on **Next** in the **Create E-Mail Notification Subscription** form.

22. In the **Recipient** section of the **Create E-Mail Notification Subscription** form, click on **Add...**.

23. Enter `peter ciso` in the filter field and click on the magnifier in the **Select objects** form.

24. Select **Peter Ciso** from the **Available objects** list and click on **Add**:

25. Click on **Next** in the **Create E-Mail Notification Subscription** form.

26. In the **Related Recipients** section of the **Create E-Mail Notification Subscription** form, click on **Next**.

27. Verify the summary in the **Create E-Mail Notification Subscription** form and click on **Create**:

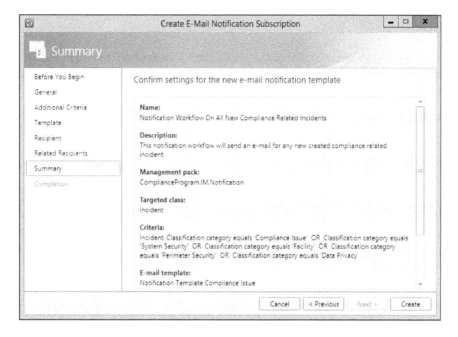

28. Click on **Close**.

29. Verify that the notification subscription is listed on the SCSM 2012 console:

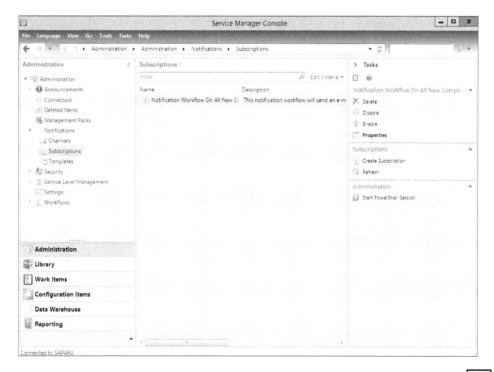

How it works...

An e-mail will be sent to the recipient of the notification subscription (to Peter Ciso in this recipe) every time an Incident is created with one of the following Incident Classification categories:

- ▸ Compliance Issue
- ▸ Compliance Issue / System Security
- ▸ Compliance Issue / Facility
- ▸ Compliance Issue / Perimeter Security
- ▸ Compliance Issue / Data Privacy

To test the notification subscription, you can create a new Incident in SCSM 2012 with one of the Compliance Issue Incident classification categories. After the Incident has been created, the notification workflow will be triggered and the e-mail will be sent to the recipient of the notification subscription.

The parameters we added in the E-Mail Notification template will be replaced by the values of the newly created incident.

The e-mail should look as follows:

A Compliance Issue Incident is created: [IR4]

SCSM Service

Gesendet: Freitag, 11. April 2014 14:17
An: Peter Ciso

Dear Peter,
A compliance related incident is logged in System Center Server Manage.
Incident ID: [IR4]
Title: Compliance Issue: Test Incident ... Notification Subscription
Description: Just a test
Please check the incident.
--- This email was sent by System Center Service Manager ---

There's more...

You can send different notifications and also send notifications to persons outside your organization.

Using different recipients for notifications related to compliance program incidents

Different recipients can be notified by e-mail based on different criteria in the notification workflow configuration. In this way, based on different requirements and Incident classifications, it is possible to notify different people who are responsible for different parts of compliance-related issues and incidents.

Notification for external personnel who are not members of the Active Directory of the organization

External personnel or groups can be notified on compliance-related incidents as well. It's possible to add a user, users, or groups manually in SCSM 2012 and add external notification e-mail addresses as well.

See also

> ▸ The *To configure email notifications* section of the Microsoft TechNet library article *How to Configure Your Infrastructure for Email Incident Support with Exchange Server 2010* at `http://technet.microsoft.com/en-us/library/jj900204.aspx`

> ▸ The Microsoft TechNet library article *How to Manually Create Configuration Items* at `http://technet.microsoft.com/en-us/library/hh495519.aspx`

Forwarding of compliance program-related alerts

The components of Microsoft System Center 2012 Operations Manager (SCOM 2012) perform different jobs and tasks. Microsoft System Center 2012 Operations Manager can be used to monitor the IT environment for compliance-related issues, as described in *Chapter 4, Monitoring the Basic Compliance Program*. Microsoft System Center 2012 Service Manager (SCSM 2012) supports IT management processes such as Incident Management, related to the **Information Technology Infrastructure Library** (**ITIL**) or **Microsoft Operational Framework** (**MOF**).

This recipe will show us how to forward a compliance program related alert, monitored in SCOM 2012, to the Incident management process in SCSM 2012.

Getting ready

To start with this recipe, you need to read the following chapters of this book:

> ▸ *Chapter 4, Monitoring the Basic Compliance Program*

> ▸ *Chapter 7, Configuring a Compliance Program in Microsoft System Center 2012 Service Manager*

▸ The *Planning the automation of the compliance management process* recipe in this chapter

How to do it...

To automatically forward compliance program related alerts in SCOM 2012 to SCSM 2012, we need to set up an Operations Manager Alert Connector in SCSM 2012 and a subscription in SCOM 2012. Perform the steps given in the following sections.

Configuring Operations Manager Alert connector in SCSM 2012

Perform the following steps to configure the Operations Manager Alert connector:

1. Open the SCSM 2012 console.

2. Navigate to **Administration | Connectors**.

3. Click on **Create connector** in the **Tasks** pane on right-hand side and choose **Operations Manager Alert Connector**:

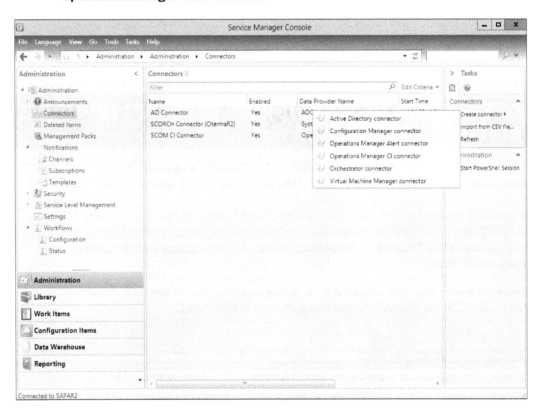

4. In the **Before You Begin** section of the **Operations Manager Alert connector** wizard form, click on **Next**.

5. Enter a name for this connector in the **Name** field of the **General** page. We will use `Ops Manager AlertConnector` as the name in our recipe.

6. Add a description in the **Description** field. This is optional but recommended.

7. Make sure the option **Enable this connector** is checked:

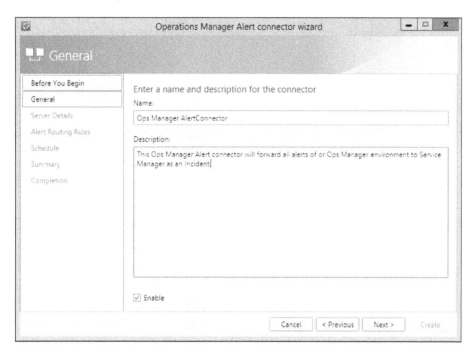

8. Click on **Next**.

9. In the **Server Details** page, specify your Operations Manager Server in the **Server name** section.

10. Add a new **Run As** account with the appropriate permissions for this connector by clicking on **New** in the **Credentials** section.

11. Fill in the required information in the **Run As Account** form:

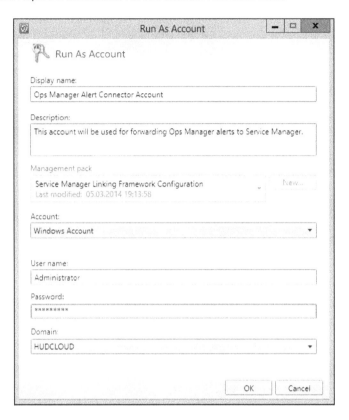

12. Click on **OK** in the **Run As Account** form.

13. Click on **Next** in the **Operations Manager Alert connector** wizard form.

14. In the **Alert Routing Rules** section, click on **Add** on the right-hand side of **Specify the routing rules for incoming alerts**.

15. In the **Add Alert Routing Rule** form, add a name for the rule in the **Rule Name** field. In our recipe, we will use `Compliance program monitor alerts`.

16. Select **Compliance Issue Incident Template** in the **Template** field (the Incident template was created in the *Creating compliance program Incident templates in System Center 2012 Service Manager* recipe of *Chapter 7, Configuring a Compliance Program in Microsoft System Center 2012 Service Manager*).

17. Check the **Operations Manager Management Pack containing the Rule or Monitor raising the alert** option.

18. Add `Compliance.program.failed.logon.events` in the field next to **Management Pack Name Equals**:

19. Click on **OK** in the **Add Alert Routing Rule** form.

20. Verify that **Operations Manager Incident Template** is selected in the **Alerts that do not fit any of the rules above will be routed with the following default template** field:

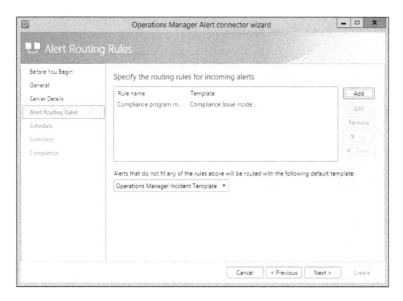

21. Click on **Next** in the **Operations Manager Alert Connector wizard** form.

22. In the **Schedule** section of the **Operations Manager Alert Connector wizard**, verify that the time for every poll alert is set to **30**.

23. Check the **Close alerts in Operations Manager when incidents are resolved or closed** option:

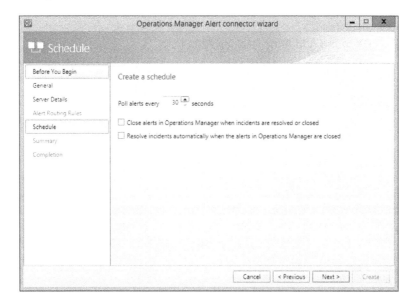

24. Click on **Next**.

25. Verify the information in the **Summary** section, click on **Create**, and then on **Close**.

Configuring the Operations Manager Alert connector in SCSM 2012

Perform the following steps to configure the Operations Manager Alert connector:

1. Open the SCOM 2012 console.

2. Navigate to **Administration | Product Connectors | Internal Connectors**:

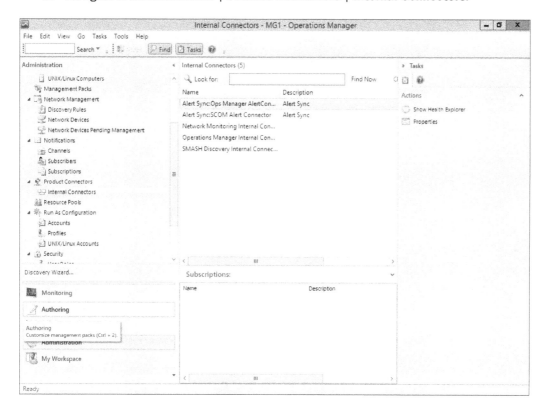

3. Double-click on the connector **Alert Sync:Ops Manager Alert Connector**; the following screen appears:

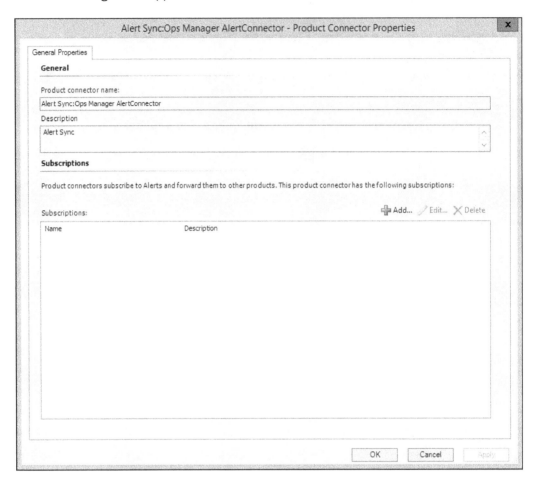

4. Click on the **+ Add** button on the right-hand side of **Subscriptions** in the **Alert Sync:Ops Manager AlertConnector – Product Connector Properties** form.

5. Add a name in the **Subscription Name** field. In this recipe, we will name it `Compliance alerts forwarding to SCSM 2012`.

6. Add some description text in the **Description** field (this is optional).

7. Click on **Next**.

8. In the **Groups** section of the **Product Connector Subscription Wizard**, uncheck the **SCOM 2012 Management Group name** option (in this environment, **MG1**).

9. Mark the checkbox next to **AD Domain Controllers (Compliance Program)**.
   This group was created in the *Adding a compliance program monitor in Microsoft System Center 2012 Operations Manager* recipe of *Chapter 4, Monitoring the Basic Compliance Program*:

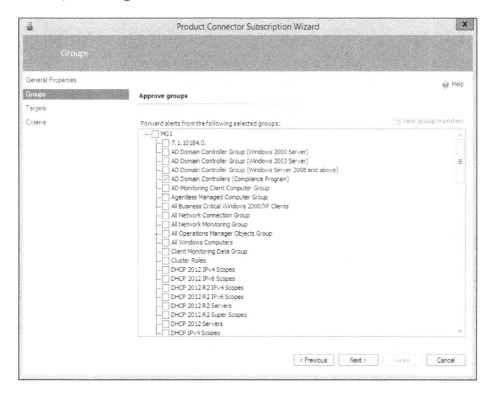

10. Click on **Next**.

11. Verify that the **Forward alerts from all targets automatically, including targets in management packs imported in the future** radio button is checked:

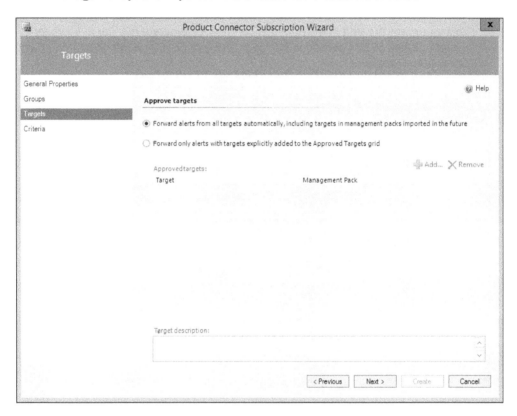

12. Click on **Next**.

13. Mark the **Error**, **Warning**, and **Information** options in the **Alerts of any of checked severity** field.

14. Mark the **High**, **Medium**, and **Low** options in the **AND any checked priority** field.

15. Mark the **New**, **Resolved**, and **Closed** options in the **AND any checked alert resolution state** field.

16. Mark all checkboxes in the **AND any checked category** field:

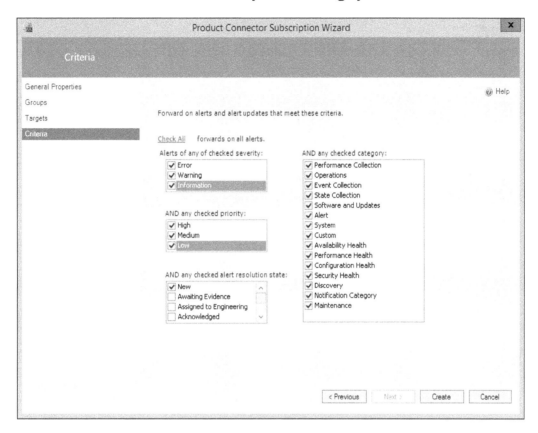

17. Click on **Create** in the **Product Connector Subscription Wizard** form.

18. Click on **OK** in the **Alert Sync:Ops Manager AlertConnector – Product Connector Properties** form:

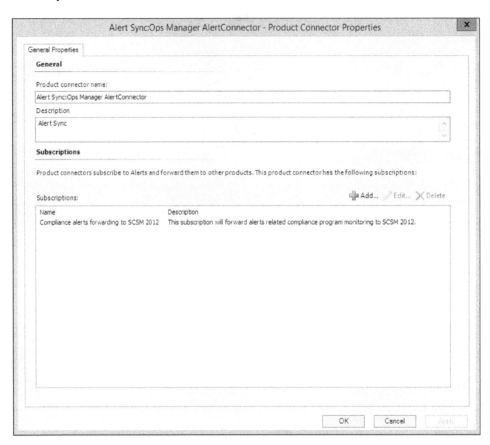

19. Click on **OK**.

How it works...

Every time a compliance-related alert is raised in SCOM 2012, which is configured and stored in the management pack named **Compliance program failed logon events**, a corresponding Incident will be created in SCSM 2012. For this incident, the SCSM 2012 Incident template **Compliance Issue Incident Template** will be applied, as shown in the following screenshot:

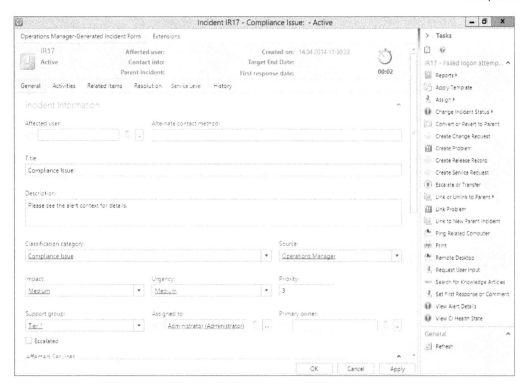

The ID and the **Assigned To** user of the Incident in SCSM 2012 will be added to the related alert in SCOM 2012:

Also, if the status of the incident in SCSM 2012 is set to **Resolved** or **Closed**, the related alert in SCOM 2012 will be marked as closed:

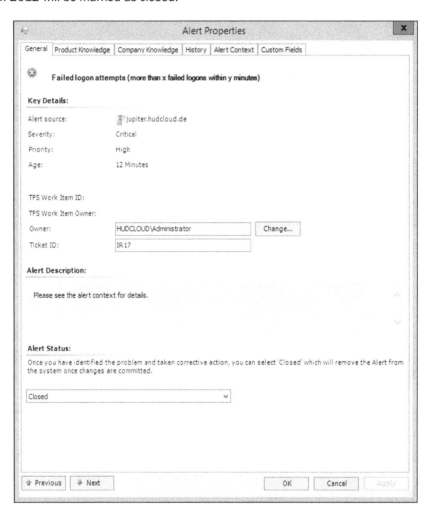

 The forwarding and syncing of alerts and Incidents between SCOM 2012 and SCSM 2012 is done by internal workflows. It might be necessary to refresh list views and forms in the SCOM 2012 and SCSM 2012 consoles to see the latest changes made by the workflows.

There's more...

More than one routing rule can be defined and alerts can be forwarded manually as well.

Defining more than one routing rule in SCSM 2012 Alert Connector

You can insert additional rules in the SCOM Alert connector in SCSM 2012 if different compliance program Incident templates need to be applied to alerts forwarded from SCOM 2012. Perform the following steps to do so:

1. Create additional Incident templates as described in the *Creating compliance program Incident templates in System Center 2012 Service Manager* recipe of *Chapter 7, Configuring a Compliance Program in Microsoft System Center 2012 Service Manager*.

2. Add rules based on the following criteria:

    ❏ Name of the management pack

    ❏ Name of the affected monitored device

3. Apply the created Incident templates based on the new rules.

> The rules in the SCOM Alert Connector in SCSM 2012 will be checked from top to down in the list. The first rule that fits by criteria will be used. Best practice is to move the most restrictive rule to first in the list. If no criterion of any rule fits the process, the default Incident template configured in the SCOM alert connector will be applied.

Manual forwarding of alerts in SCOM 2012 to SCSM 2012

It is possible to forward alerts from SCOM 2012 to SCSM 2012 manually as well. This might be necessary if you don't have a subscription in SCOM for forwarding or if you don't have a configured rule in this subscription that fits the criteria.

Perform the following steps to forward an alert from SCOM 2012 to SCSM 2012 manually:

1. Open the SCOM 2012 console.

2. Navigate to **Monitoring | Active Alerts**.

3. Right-click on an alert in the middle view pane of the SCOM 2012 console.

4. Choose **Forward to** alert from the context menu:

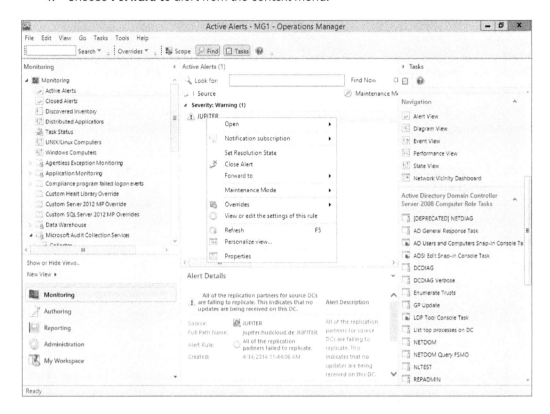

5. Click on **Alert Sync:Ops Manager AlertConnector**:

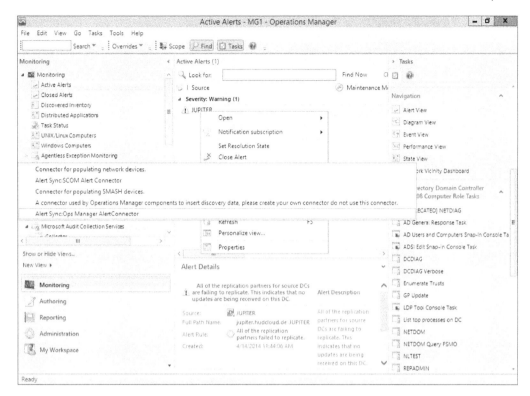

The preceding steps will manually forward the marked alert to SCSM 2012 and an Incident will be created based on the routing rules configured in the **Operations Manager Alert Connector**.

See also

► http://technet.microsoft.com/en-us/library/hh519707.aspx (the *How to Import Management Packs for System Center Operations Manager Configuration Item Connectors* article in Microsoft TechNet library)

Forwarding compliance program-related Compliance Settings Management issues

In Microsoft System Center 2012 Configuration Manager (SCCM 2012), a baseline can be configured in Compliance Settings Management. If SCCM 2012 detects a drift of the compliance program baseline, this issue can be forwarded to SCSM 2012 to automatically create a corresponding Incident.

Getting ready

To start this recipe, you need to read the following chapters and recipes in this book:

▶   *Chapter 3, Enhancing the Basic Compliance Program Using Microsoft System Center 2012 Configuration Manager*

▶   *Chapter 7, Configuring a Compliance Program in Microsoft System Center 2012 Service Manager*

▶   The *Planning the automation of the compliance management process* recipe of this chapter

 Verify that the SCCM Connector in SCSM 2012 has been completed successfully before starting with this recipe.

How to do it...

To configure the automatic forwarding of compliance issues tracked by SCCM 2012 Compliance Settings Management, perform the following steps:

1.   Open the SCSM 2012 console.

2.   Navigate to **Administration** | **Configuration**.

3.   Double-click on **Desired Configuration Management Event Workflow Configuration** in the middle pane of the SCSM 2012 console:

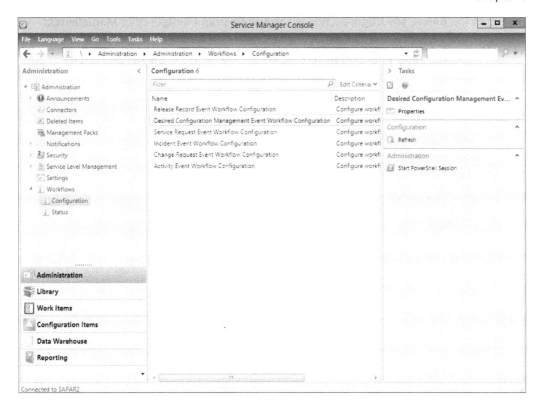

4. Click on **Add** in the **Configure Desired Configuration Management Workflows** form. The following screen should appear:

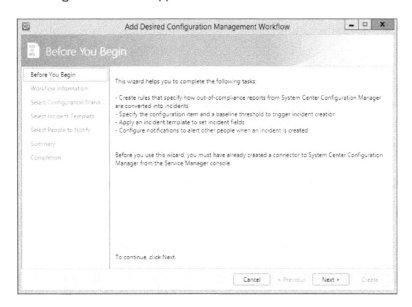

5. In the **Before You Begin** section of the **Add Desired Configuration Management Workflow** form, click on **Next**.

6. In the **Workflow Information** section, enter a name in the **Name** field. In this recipe, SCCM Compliance Settings Workflow is used.

7. Enter a description in the **Description (optional)** field.

8. Click on **New...** next to the **Management Pack** field.

9. In the **Create Management Pack** form, enter a name and a description (optional). In this recipe, ComplianceProgram.IM.SCCMComplianceSettingsWorkflows is used:

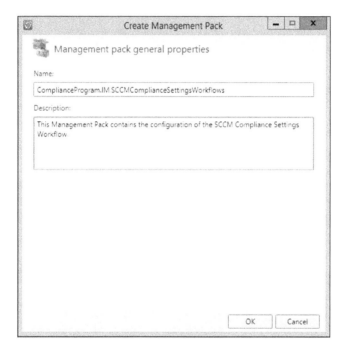

10. Click on **OK** in the **Create Management Pack** form.

11. Verify that the Management Pack, **ComplianceProgram.IM.SCCMComplianceSettings Workflows**, is selected and the **Enabled** checkbox is selected:

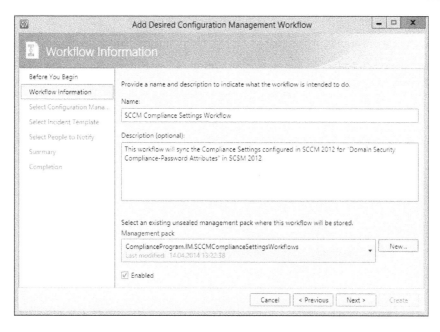

12. Click on **Next**.

13. In the **Select System Center Configuration Manager Configuration Items** section, select the sub-entry, **Domain Security Compliance-Password Attributes**, below the **WS2012 Domain Security Compliance** entry:

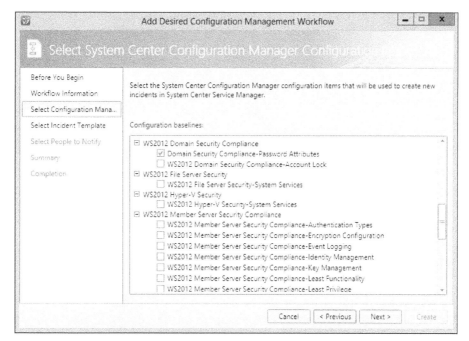

14. Click on **Next**.

15. In the **Select Incident Template** section, click on **Apply the following template**.

16. Select the **Compliance Issue Incident Template** (the Incident template was created in the *Creating compliance program Incident templates in System Center 2012 Service Manager* recipe of *Chapter 7, Configuring a Compliance Program in Microsoft System Center 2012 Service Manager*):

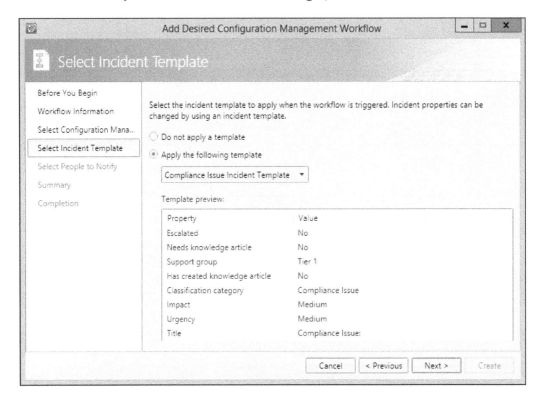

17. Click on **Next**.

18. In the **Select People to Notify** section of the **Add Desired Configuration Management Workflow** form, click on **Next**.

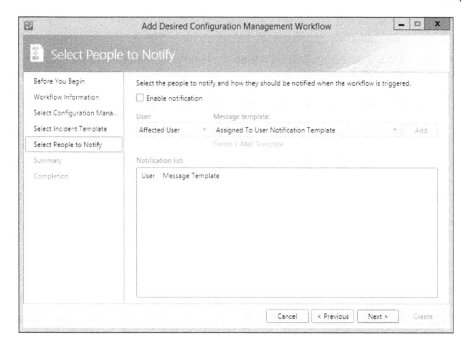

19. Verify the **Summary** page and click on **Create**.
20. Click on **Close**.
21. Click on **OK** in the **Configure Desired Configuration Management Workflow** form:

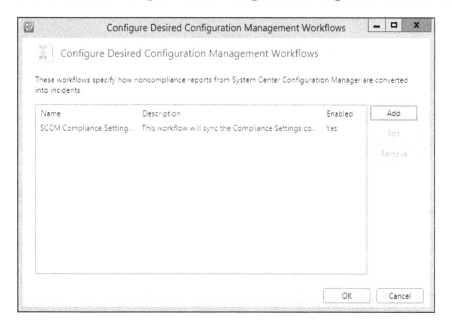

How it works...

Every time SCCM 2012 detects a drift on a system covered by the compliance program baseline, an incident will be created automatically in SCSM 2012 based on the predefined Incident template.

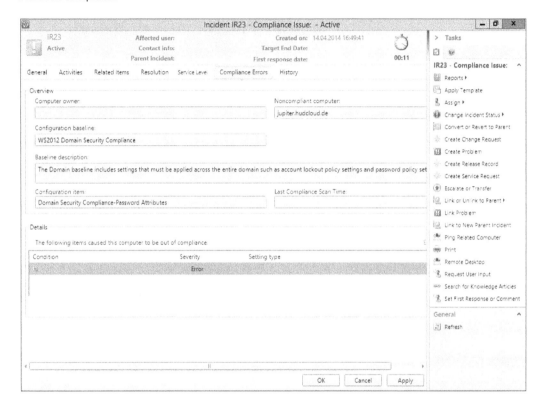

There's more...

You can add more than one workflow to forward Compliance Settings Management issues from SCCSM to SCSM 2012.

Adding more than one workflow to forward Compliance Settings Management issues from SCCM 2012 to SCSM 2012

You can create more than one workflow in SCSM 2012 to create Incidents based on Compliance Settings Management issues. This offers the option of applying different Incident templates with different details to the created Incident record; for instance, to route the Incident to different support groups or set different priorities to this Incident. Repeat the steps in the *How to do it...* section of this recipe and choose individual criteria and different Incident templates to achieve this.

See also

▶ `http://technet.microsoft.com/en-us/library/hh495612.aspx` (the Microsoft TechNet library article *Configuring Desired Configuration Management to Generate Incidents in System Center 2012 - Service Manager*)

9
Reporting on Compliance with System Center 2012

In this chapter, we will cover the following topics:

- ▶ Planning compliance reporting in Microsoft System Center 2012

- ▶ Generating compliance program reports in Microsoft System Center 2012 Configuration Manager

- ▶ Generating compliance program reports in Microsoft System Center 2012 Operations Manager Audit Collection Service

- ▶ Generating compliance program reports in Microsoft System Center 2012 Service Manager

Introduction

Reports provide a view of your company's current compliance status. They are key to a successful compliance program. Based on the information provided by compliance reports, companies can decide when further activities are necessary. Reports should provide answers and achieve specific company objectives. If they don't meet a specific goal, they can be a waste of time and, more importantly, of money. Avoid creating reports just for the sake of having reports. Unnecessary reports can create a false sense of security. Of course, you may be able to tick the checkbox on your project plan that says you are compliant with your access policy but, if no one uses those reports, then no one will react to a compliance issue when it occurs. So your company may believe that everything is OK as you have those reports while in reality your system becomes non-compliant.

This chapter focuses on the considerations for a reporting process and the kind of reports the System Center products provide. The first recipe is the basis for the following recipes. It details what is required to create reports. The following three recipes provide hands-on examples on how to create compliance reports using the various System Center tools.

In order to work through this chapter, the following chapters should be completed:

- Chapter 3, *Enhancing the Basic Compliance Program Using Microsoft System Center 2012 Configuration Manager*
- Chapter 4, *Monitoring the Basic Compliance Program*
- Chapter 6, *Planning a Compliance Program in Microsoft System Center 2012*
- Chapter 7, *Configuring a Compliance Program in Microsoft System Center 2012 Service Manager*

Planning compliance reporting in Microsoft System Center 2012

It is not enough to decide just what is to be reported. You must also consider the architecture of your reporting system and the security of your input information and the reports themselves. This recipe provides examples on what considerations should be made for compliance reporting.

Getting ready

In *Chapter 6, Planning a Compliance Program in Microsoft System Center 2012*, we talked about the types of reports, the importance of the input/output, and when to use System Center products. You should have worked through *Chapter 6, Planning a Compliance Program in Microsoft System Center 2012*, especially through the recipe *Planning and defining compliance reports*.

In addition, valuable information on input data, report structure, stakeholders, and much more is provided in an upcoming cookbook by author Sam Erskine from Packt Publishing. This book on System Center Reporting will cover each of the products in the System Center family we discussed.

How to do it...

As mentioned in *Chapter 6, Planning a Compliance Program in Microsoft System Center 2012*, several regulatory requirements demand reports or monitoring of controls in addition to audits of your compliance program. There are several important factors to be considered for reports to be acceptable for audits. The minimum factors for considerations should be as follows:

- Secure the input data for your reports

- Secure and audit the reporting system
- Also, if required/possible, archive the report information (input)

Input data for reports must be secured in order for it to be considered as a reliable data source. For example, logs are only reliable if they cannot be easily manipulated. When deciding on an automated tool for controls, and therefore an input source for your reports, always review input sources for vulnerabilities and, when required, implement protection. The same holds true for your reporting system. It must include protective measures to ensure the reliability of your reports. The most common measures are as follows:

- Independent audit trail
- Segregation of duty
- Non-volatile activity history
- Archiving of input data and/or reports

To use a structured approach, you should carry out the following steps:

1. Identify and document input data (or a reporting system).
2. Identify and document regulatory requirements on input data, reports, and reporting systems.
3. Identify and document protective measures for your input data (or reports in your reporting system) — do this keeping the three principles of confidentiality, integrity, and availability in mind.
4. Define further measures if the results of step 3 are not adequate (optional).
5. Implement those measures (optional).

To go through these steps, you must understand what you want to protect your input data and reporting system from. The following table provides examples of the possible measurements mentioned previously and connects them with the System Center products:

Target	Measures	Description
Input data Example: Windows server event logs	Integrity: Automatic copy of logs to the System Center Operations Manager (SCOM) ACS	Manipulation of logs by Windows server administrators is prevented as SCOM copies input data logs to its own system right away
Input data Example: Windows server event logs	Confidentiality: Segregation of the duties implemented in System Center Operations Manager	To ensure only relevant users have access to logs/reports, SCOM ACS has its own database and account management; so even a full SCOM administrator has no access to logs

Target	Measures	Description
Input data Example: Windows server event logs	Availability: Relevant information of logs required for reports are archived in the SCOM ACS	Even if original logs are deleted or overwritten, input data of logs is available in the SCOM ACS for a predefined length of time
Reports in the reporting system	Integrity: All System Center products provide non-volatile activity history	To ensure that no reports or input data have been manipulated; activity histories are essential
Reporting system	Integrity: All System Center products have an audit trail (regulatory requirement)	Ensure that the system has not been manipulated by reviewing the audit trail or creating controls

Follow the previous steps even if you use tools other than System Center. You have to consider them as there are many regulatory and internal requirements that must be followed. For example, PCI DSS demands an audit trail of input data and reports. So, historical information must be available to show how the results of the report have been created. This might mean that input data, such as the logs that SCOM ACS uses for its reports, have to be archived. SCOM ACS does this automatically for the configured time period. Other System Center tools also save the information that is pulled automatically via agents into their databases. SCCM saves audit trail information these 180 days by default.

In addition, reports run on controls should be saved. If a control demands monthly reports, an auditor may ask you to provide the results from February of this year. You have to be able to provide this information straightaway. Therefore, when generating reports using System Center products or other tools, it might be a good idea to save the reports to an external path in addition to the information on the actions you performed based on these reports. In this case, secure the location of the reports and remediation steps you took, so that only the need-to-know people have access. Keep in mind, sensitive information could be included in these reports. Use the control from *Chapter 4, Monitoring the Basic Compliance Program*, related to Object Access, to ensure no unauthorized access has occurred.

How it works...

Perform the steps described in this recipe to ensure the reliability of your reports. Confirm that the input data is secured and that reports are stored in a secure way. Also, make sure that the report system is audited to ensure that no manipulation has taken place.

Generating compliance program reports in Microsoft System Center 2012 Configuration Manager

Chapter 3, Enhancing the Basic Compliance Program Using Microsoft System Center 2012 Configuration Manager, provided information on how to configure Microsoft System Center 2012 Configuration Manager to create a compliance program. This recipe will focus on how to generate compliance reports based on the data collected/created in *Chapter 3, Enhancing the Basic Compliance Program Using Microsoft System Center 2012 Configuration Manager*.

Getting ready

The prerequisites for this recipe are:

- An installed Microsoft System Center 2012 Configuration Manager environment. This includes:
    - SCCM 2012 Configuration Manager Server

- In addition, the following recipes from *Chapter 3, Enhancing the Basic Compliance Program Using Microsoft System Center 2012 Configuration Manager*, should be finished before starting with this recipe:
    - *Configuring Microsoft System Center 2012 Configuration Manager for compliance*
    - *Using Security Compliance Manager baselines in Microsoft System Center 2012 Configuration Manager*

 All recipes should work with System Center 2012 Configuration Manager, System Center 2012 SP1 Configuration Manager, and System Center 2012 R2 Configuration Manager.

How to do it...

To run an SCCM 2012 report, perform the following steps:

1. Open the SCCM 2012 console.
2. Navigate to **Monitoring**.
3. In the navigation menu, go to **Reporting** and open it.
4. Click on **Reports** to open it.

5. Choose the category **Compliance and Settings Management**, as all compliance reports belong to this category:

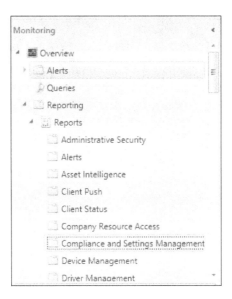

6. Select the required report. Here, as an example, **Summary compliance of a configuration baseline for a collection** is selected:

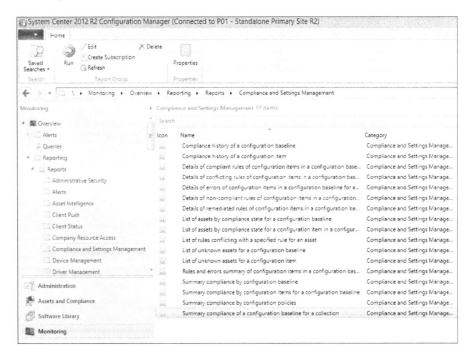

7. On the ribbon on top of the console, click on **Run**. The **Summary compliance of a configuration baseline for a collection** report launches.

8. A new window opens—all input variables that are required have a red highlighted exclamation point. Click on **Values...** to provide the information:

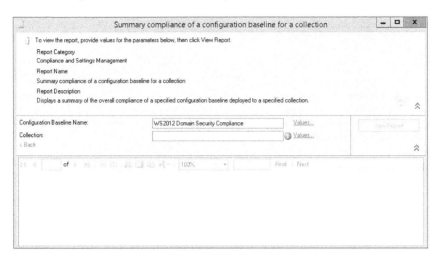

9. Click on **Values** beside **Configuration Baseline Names**:

10. A new window opens where all baselines are provided. Based on *Chapter 3, Enhancing the Basic Compliance Program Using Microsoft System Center 2012 Configuration Manager*, you should have created a compliance baseline. Choose the created baseline here. Here we select the baseline **WS2012 Domain Security Compliance** and then click on the **OK** button:

11. Beside **Collection**, click on **Values....** In the new window, all collections are provided. Click on **All Systems** and then on **OK**.

12. Click on **View Report**:

13. The report opens, providing an overview of the compliance status for all configured controls within this configuration baseline.

How it works...

This default summary report provides all controls that are part of this configuration baseline. In *Chapter 3, Enhancing the Basic Compliance Program Using Microsoft System Center 2012 Configuration Manager*, we created two controls — one for password compliance and one for account lockout compliance. Both controls were added within the WS2012 Domain Security Compliance baseline.

The afore mentioned compliance reports are based on the configuration baseline created in System Center Configuration Manager. Before creating a compliance baseline, consider the information you require within a certain report. So, in this case, as both compliance controls center around the access policy compliance based on Active Directory, they were put in the same baseline.

This is just one report provided by SCCM 2012. Depending on your requirements, a different report might provide more value for meeting your reporting goals.

There's more...

The report shown in this recipe provides only summarized information. This is great for certain stakeholders, but the compliance team or the team responsible for remediation requires further information. Many out-of-the-box System Center reports are dynamic and provide further information. The System Center products provide further functionalities too.

Getting details on the configuration baselines and affected systems

The summary report provides further information that is of interest to the compliance and security/audit teams. Several values are underlined within the reports. These values provide further details.

To understand which controls are part of the configuration baseline WS2012 Domain Security Compliance and to know their actual compliance status, do the following:

1. Run a report as described in the *How to do it...* section of this recipe.

2. Beside **Configuration Baseline Name**, click on **WS2012 Domain Security Compliance**. A new report is created:

3. Click on the Save icon to save this report.

This report provides information on the two controls. The information provided on those controls includes the compliance status, number of failed systems, number of remediated systems, number of not-detected systems, severity, and so on. All the listed values are links to further details.

If you want to understand which systems are noncompliant, click on the number under **Non-Compliant** and a new report will be created with a list of all the noncompliant systems.

Creating scheduled reports

It is possible to schedule reports. Some regulatory requirements demand that reports be run at certain time intervals. In addition, most internal security compliance requirements demand quarterly, monthly, or, for very critical controls, even weekly reports or audit trails.

To create a scheduled report, perform the following steps:

1. Open the SCCM 2012 R2 console.

2. Navigate to **Monitoring**.

3. In the navigation menu, go to **Reporting** and open it.

4. Click on **Reports** to open it.

5. Choose the **Compliance and Settings Management** category as all compliance reports belong to this category.

6. In the ribbon at the top, select **Create Subscription**:

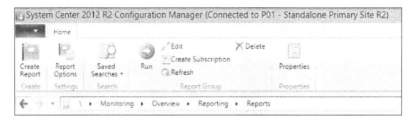

7. A new window appears. All the values with exclamation points must be entered. Thus, provide values for the **File Name** and **Path** fields to specify where to store the report, supply values for **User Name** and **Password**, specify how many reports to store (overwrite or not), and then click on **Next**:

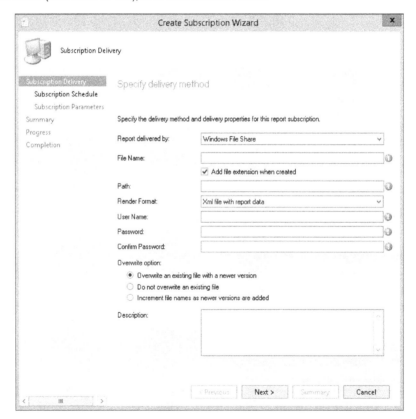

8. In the next window, define the report schedule interval. To create a schedule, define the interval as hourly, daily, weekly, monthly, or once. Depending on the interval, different options are possible. For example, monthly intervals could be run every first Sunday of the month or on the 21st day of each month. A similar schedule could be run on a quarterly or weekly basis:

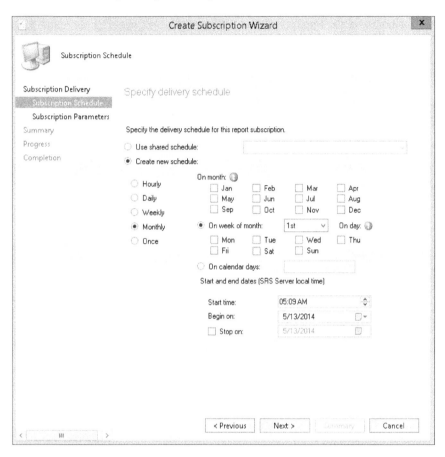

9. Next, the configuration baseline and collection that should provide the input values for this report must be selected. In our case, this would be the same as in the example used in the *How to do it...* section.

10. The summary page provides an overview of all settings. After that, the schedule will be created.

Generating compliance program reports in Microsoft System Center 2012 Operations Manager Audit Collection Service

In *Chapter 4, Monitoring the Basic Compliance Program*, we configured Microsoft **System Center 2012 Operations Manager Audit Collection Service** (**SCOM 2012 ACS**) to collect compliance program data based on object access. This recipe will show you how to generate a compliance program report based on the data collected by SCOM 2012 ACS.

Getting ready

The prerequisites for this recipe are as follows:

- An installation of Microsoft System Center 2012 Operations Manager Audit Collection Services environment. This includes:
    - SCOM 2012 Management Server with Audit Collection Service

- Also, the following recipes of *Chapter 4, Monitoring the Basic Compliance Program*, should be finished before starting with this recipe:
    - *Installing Microsoft System Center 2012 Operations Manager Audit Collection Services to support the compliance program*
    - *Configuring a compliance program in Microsoft System Center 2012 Operations Manager Audit Collection Services*

> All recipes should work with System Center 2012 Operations Manager, System Center 2012 SP1 Operations Manager, and System Center 2012 R2 Operations Manager.

How to do it...

To run an SCOM 2012 ACS report, perform the following steps:

1. Open **Internet Explorer** (**IE**) on a computer connected to the same network as the SCOM 2012 ACS server.

2. Type the URL of the SCOM 2012 ACS Reporting Service in the address field. In this recipe, the URL will be `http://SCOM2012R2ACS/Reports`. Press the *Enter* key:

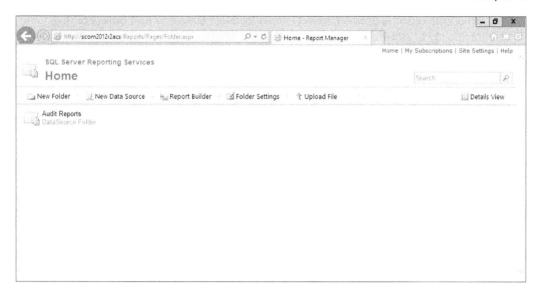

3. Click on **Audit Reports** in the IE.

4. Click on the **Usage _-_Object_Access** report to open the report:

5. When the report is opened, select values for **Start Date** and **End Date**. For this recipe, **1/1/2014** is used as the **Start Date** and the current date as the **End Date** for the report.

6. Click on **View Report**.

7. Click on the arrows near the word **Path** in the report:

8. Scroll in the report to the folder defined in the planning phase of *Chapter 4, Monitoring the Basic Compliance Program*. In this recipe, it is `C:\Data`:

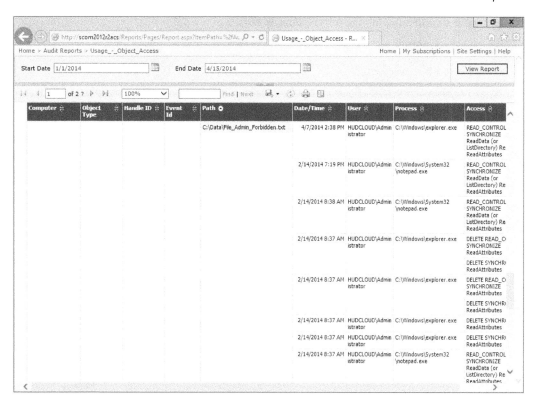

How it works...

The default report will show all events that are logged in the SCOM 2012 Audit Collection Service related to the object access. Object access is any access to a file or folder that was specified in the configuration in the *Configuring a compliance program in Microsoft System Center 2012 Operations Manager Audit Collection Services* recipe of *Chapter 4, Monitoring the Basic Compliance Program*.

There's more...

To archive the report for a later compliance audit, it is possible to save the report in different formats.

Saving the SCOM 2012 ACS compliance program report in a different format

It is possible to save the SCOM 2012 ACS report in a different file format and archive the file for later use in compliance program audits.

To save the report in a file, perform the following steps:

1. Run a report as described in the *How to do it...* section of this recipe.

2. Click on the disk icon.

3. Choose a file format you want to save the report in. In this recipe, the **PDF** format has been used:

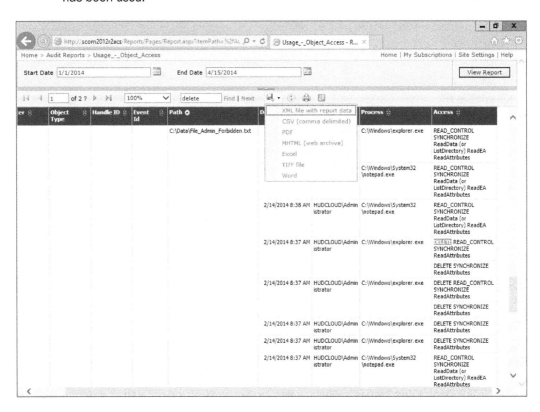

4. In the dialog window, click on the arrow next to **Save** and then click on **Save as**:

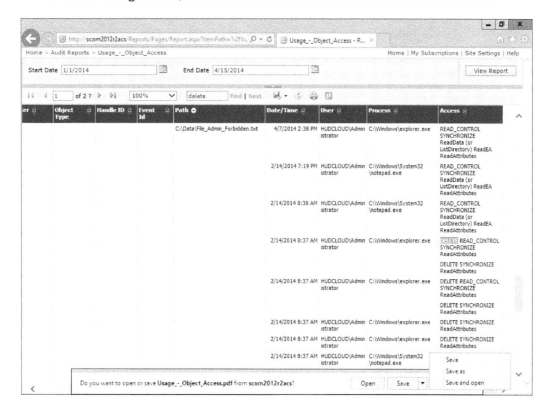

5. In the **Save As** dialog box, navigate to a folder. In this recipe, `C:\Audit_Data` is used.

6. Specify a name for the file in the **File name** field. In this recipe, `Audit_File-Access.pdf` is the name used:

7. Click on **Save**.

See also

▶ `http://technet.microsoft.com/en-us/library/hh528528.aspx` (the Microsoft TechNet library article *Report Authoring for System Center 2012 – Operations Manager*)

Generating compliance program reports in Microsoft System Center 2012 Service Manager

In *Chapter 7, Configuring a Compliance Program in Microsoft System Center 2012 Service Manager,* we configured SCSM 2012 to support the compliance program management process based on Incident Management. This recipe will show how compliance-program-related reports in SCSM 2012 can be generated.

Getting ready

The prerequisites for all following recipes are as follows:

- An installed Microsoft System Center 2012 Service Manager environment. This includes:
    - SCSM 2012 Management Server
    - SCSM 2012 Data Warehouse Server
    - SCSM 2012 Self-Service Portal (optional)

- The following recipes in *Chapter 7, Configuring a Compliance Program in Microsoft System Center 2012 Service Manager* should be read:
    - *Configuring compliance process Incident Classification Categories in System Center 2012 Service Manager*
    - *Creating compliance program Incident templates in System Center 2012 Service Manager*

- You should have some Incidents created in SCSM 2012 with one of the following classification categories:
    - **Compliance Issue**
    - **Compliance Issue / System Security**
    - **Compliance Issue / Facility**
    - **Compliance Issue / Perimeter Security**
    - **Compliance Issue / Data Privacy**

 All recipes should work with System Center 2012 Server Manager, System Center 2012 SP1 Service Manager, and System Center 2012 R2 Service Manager.

How to do it...

To run a SCSM 2012 compliance program, perform the following steps:

1. Open the SCSM 2012 console.

2. Navigate to **Reporting** | **Reports** | **Incident Management**:

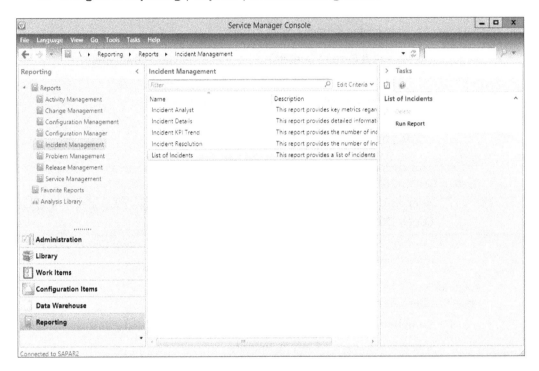

3. Double-click on the **List of Incidents** report; the following screen appears:

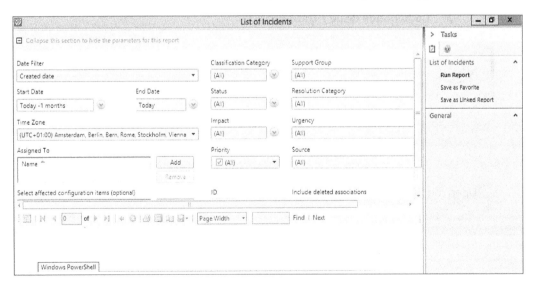

4. When the report is opened, select values for the **Start Date** and **End Date** of the report. For this recipe, select **First day of this year** by clicking on the button below the **Start Date** field and the current date as the **End Date** for the report.

5. Expand the **Classification Category** list by clicking on the button next to it.

6. Unmark the checkbox at **All**.

7. Expand the **Compliance Issue** list entry.

8. Tick the checkboxes for **Compliance Issue**, **Data Privacy**, **Facility**, **Perimeter Security**, and **System Security**:

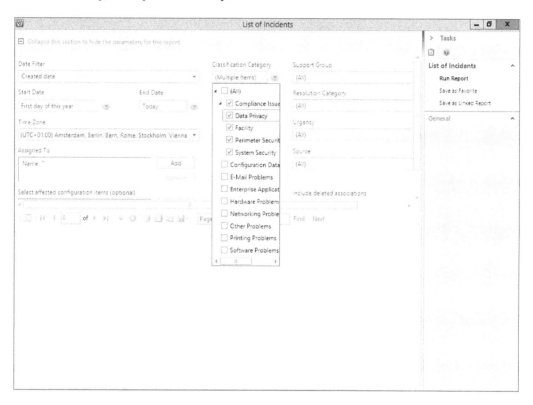

9. On the **Tasks** pane at the right-hand side of the SCSM 2012 console, click on **Run Report**:

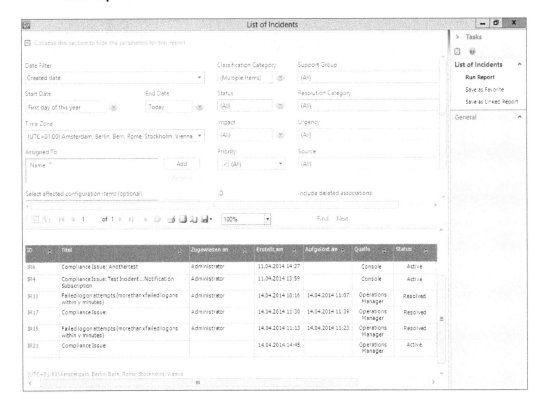

How it works...

Based on the filters, the list of incidents in the report will be created.

The result of the compliance program report shows all Incidents logged in SCSM 2012 with the following criteria:

▶ The incident is created on or later than the first day of the current year until the current date

    And

▶ The incident **Classification Category** equals any one of the following:

    ❏ **Compliance Issue**

    Or

    ❏ **Compliance Issue / System Security**

Or

❏ **Compliance Issue / Facility**

Or

❏ **Compliance Issue / Perimeter Security**

Or

❏ **Compliance Issue / Data Privacy**

There's more...

Sometimes, it is necessary to see the details of a compliance-related incident. Another requirement is to run the report with the same filter settings again. Both requirements can be met.

Getting the details of an incident in the List of Incidents report

To get a detailed view of an Incident in the **List of Incidents** report, click on the Incident **ID** in the first column of the generated compliance program report.

All details of the selected Incident will be shown in the report detail pane.

Saving the configured filters of the List of Incidents report as a Favorite

Instead of configuring the filters of the **List of Incidents** report every time you need the compliance program report, you can save the filter settings as a Favorite report in the SCSM 2012 console. Perform the following steps to save an annual compliance program report as a Favorite:

1. Configure the filter as shown in the *How to do it...* section of this recipe.
2. Run the report by clicking on **Run Report** in the **Tasks** pane.
3. Verify that the result set meets your requirements.
4. Click on **Save as Favorite** in the **Tasks** pane on the right-hand side.
5. Enter a name in the **Save favorite report** window, for example, `Incident Compliance Report (Current year)`, and click on **OK**:

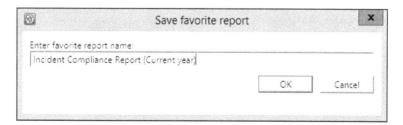

6. In the SCSM console, navigate to **Reporting | Favorite Reports**.

7. The created Favorite report is listed and is ready for use:

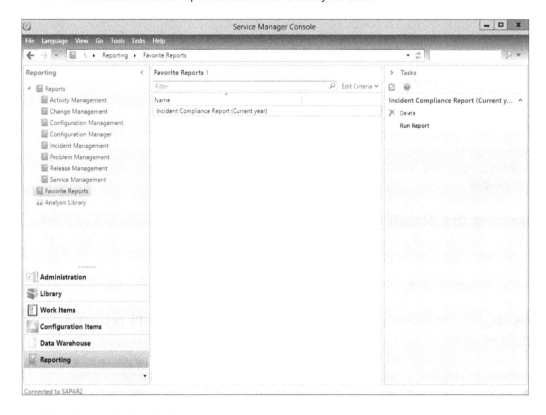

See also

▶ http://technet.microsoft.com/en-us/library/hh519671.aspx (the Microsoft TechNet library article *Using Data Warehouse Reporting and Analytics in System Center 2012 – Service Manager*)

Useful Websites and Community Resources

Introduction

System Center has a large community of partners and IT professionals who, along with the product developers, contribute to constant advancement and innovation. This book is part of a vast pool of information available to readers, and this appendix will list some helpful websites and communities for System Center 2012.

Just as with technology, compliance requirements change. New frameworks or tools are provided to help with the creation of compliance programs. This appendix will provide links to some of those frameworks and regulatory requirement websites.

We recommend you bookmark the sites and follow the blogs to enhance your knowledge with free resources.

Compliance and System Center Partner tools

- **Derdack**: http://www.derdack.com/microsoftsco
- **Cireson**: http://cireson.com
- **Provance**: http://www.provance.com/products/provance-it-asset-management-pack/overview
- **OpsLogix**: http://www.opslogix.com/
- **BSI GSTOOL** (https://www.bsi.bund.de/DE/Themen/weitereThemen/GSTOOL/gstool.html;jsessionid=C4CD396BB70A2906FF3346FA422BEC3C.2_cid286)

Authors' community blogs

- **Susan Roesner (German)**: http://startblog.hud.de/
- **Andreas Baumgarten (German)**: http://startblog.hud.de/
- **Ronnie Isherwood**: http://virtualfat.com

Useful System Center community blogs

- **System Center Team Blog:** http://blogs.technet.com/b/systemcenter/
- **System Center Operations Manager Engineering Blog**: http://blogs.technet.com/b/momteam/
- **System Center: Service Manager Engineering Blog**: http://blogs.technet.com/b/servicemanager/
- **System Center Configuration Manager Team Blog**: http://blogs.technet.com/b/configmgrteam/
- **Steve Beaumont**: http://systemscentre.blogspot.co.uk/
- **Samuel Erskine**: http://itprocessed.com/
- **Kurt van Hoecke (MVP)**: http://scug.be/
- **Marcel Zehner (MVP)**: http://blog.scsmfaq.ch/
- **Anton Grisenko (MVP)**: http://blog.scsmsolutions.com/
- **Patrik Sundqvist (MVP)**: http://litware.se/
- **Nathan Lasnosk (MVP)**: http://blog.concurrency.com/author/nlasnoski/
- **Anders Bengtsson**: http://contoso.se/blog/

Useful Security/Compliance community blogs

- **SANS.org (resources and training on security, especially the top 20 critical controls)**: http://www.sans.org/security-resources/
- **Internet Storm Center**: https://isc.sans.edu/diary.html
- **Securities Exchange Commissions (SEC)**: http://www.sec.gov/rules.shtml
- **Resources under news/studies**: http://www.sec.gov/index.htm
- **General regulatory information**: http://msdn.microsoft.com/en-us/library/aa480484.aspx

Frameworks, standards, and processes

► Regulatory requirements mentioned in *Chapter 2, Implementing the First Steps of Basic Compliance*:

□ **Sarbanes Oxley Act (SOX)**: http://www.gpo.gov/fdsys/pkg/PLAW-107publ204/content-detail.html

□ **Payment Card Industry Data Security Standard (PCI DSS)**: https://www.pcisecuritystandards.org/

□ **Example to PCI DSS based on Windows Azure**: http://go.microsoft.com/fwlink/?LinkId=389876

□ **Bundesdatenschutzgesetz (BDSG)**: http://www.bfdi.bund.de/cae/servlet/contentblob/409518/publicationFile/25234/BDSG.pdf

► **Official ITIL website**: http://www.itil-officialsite.com/

► **Microsoft Operations Framework**: http://technet.microsoft.com/en-us/library/cc506049.aspx

► **ISO official website**: http://www.iso.org/iso/home.html

► **Unified Compliance Framework**: https://www.unifiedcompliance.com/

► **German BSI**: https://www.bsi.bund.de/DE/Themen/ITGrundschutz/ITGrundschutzInternational/intl.html

► **Auditing Standard SSAE 16 Reporting Standard (enhancement of SAS70) especially enhanced for Cloud solutions and outsourcing**: http://www.ssae-16.com/

Official websites on compliance requirements

► **US (for small businesses)**: http://www.sba.gov/

► **UK (a starting point for businesses, which includes information on tax and export compliance)**: https://www.gov.uk/

► **Australia**: http://www.standards.org.au/Pages/default.aspx

Valuable community forums and user groups

► **TechNet Forums – Compliance Management EN**: http://social.technet.microsoft.com/Forums/en-US/home?forum=compliancemanagement

► **TechNet Forums – System Center Operations Manager (EN)**: http://social.technet.microsoft.com/Forums/systemcenter/en-US/home?forum=operationsmanagergeneral

- **TechNet Forums – System Center Service Manager (EN)**: `http://social.technet.microsoft.com/Forums/systemcenter/en-US/home?category=servicemanager`

- **TechNet Forums – System Center Configuration Manager EN**: `http://social.technet.microsoft.com/Forums/en-us/home?category=systemcenter2012configurationmanager`

- **TechNet Forums – System Center (DE)**: `http://social.technet.microsoft.com/Forums/de-DE/systemcenterde/threads`

- **SCSM.US**: `http://scsm.us/`

- **German System Center User Group**: `http://scsmug.de/`

- **German Private Cloud User Group**: `http://www.building-clouds.de/`

Microsoft TechNet Information

- **Collecting Security Events for Audits in Operations Manager**: `http://technet.microsoft.com/en-us/library/hh212908.aspx`

- **Compliance Settings in Configuration Manager**: `http://technet.microsoft.com/en-us/library/gg682139.aspx`

- **Microsoft Security Compliance Manager**: `http://technet.microsoft.com/en-us/library/cc677002.aspx`

- **Microsoft TechNet Wiki - Management Portal**: `http://social.technet.microsoft.com/wiki/contents/articles/703.wiki-management-portal.aspx`

- **Security baselines for Windows 8.1, Windows Server 2012 and Internet Explorer 11**: `http://blogs.technet.com/b/secguide/archive/2014/04/07/security-baselines-for-windows-8-1-windows-server-2012-r2-and-internet-explorer-11.aspx`

Social network resources

- **System Center on Facebook**: `https://www.facebook.com/pages/Microsoft-System-Center-Support/111513322193410`

- **System Center on Twitter**: `https://twitter.com/system_center`

Index

N

Network Vicinity Dashboard
  about 12
  viewing 12
notification template
  creating, for compliance issue notification
      e-mails 192-197

O

Operations Manager 2012
  importing, steps 159, 160
Operations Manager Alert connector
  configuring, in SCSM 2012 206-218
Operations Manager CI connector
  configuring 166-168
Organizational Unit (OU)
  about 27
  design considerations 28

P

Password GPO baseline
  implementing 48
**Payment Card Industry Data Security
    Standard (PCI DSS)**
  about 11, 76
  URL 76
plan-do-check-act (PDCA) cycle 114
preventive controls 14
project management
  using, in compliance approach 111
project prioritization 117
project structure
  defining 114

R

remediation, noncompliance
  primary owner 147
Remote Connection Profiles 62
Reporting services point site system role 53
risk assessment approach
  planning 120-125
role-based access control 21
routing rules
  defining, in SCSM 2012 Alert Connector 219

S

SCCM 2012
  compliance program reports,
    generating in 235-238
scheduled reports
  creating 239-241
SCOM
  about 75
  URL 76
SCOM 2012 ACS
  compliance program report, saving in different
    format 245-248
  compliance program reports,
    generating in 242-245
SCOM 2012 to SCSM 2012
  manual forwarding, of alerts 219-221
  workflows, adding to forward Compliance
    Settings Management issues 228
SCOM ACS
  ACS Filter, creating on 100
SCOM ACS database
  audit data, checking 106, 107
SCOM ACS server
  auditing filter, checking 105
scope, compliance program
  logical scope 10
  physical scope 10
  planning 8, 9
scope definition
  defining, by business 9
  defining, by requirements 10, 11
  example 11
SCSM
  multiple connectors, adding 169
SCSM 2012
  about 157
  classes, adding 173
  compliance process Incident Classification
    Categories, configuring in 173-176
  compliance program, running 249-253
  compliance program Change Request
    templates, creating in 184, 185
  compliance program Incident templates,
    creating 180-183
  compliance program notification,
    configuring in 191, 192

Thank you for buying
Microsoft System Center 2012 R2 Compliance Management Cookbook

About Packt Publishing

Packt, pronounced 'packed', published its first book "*Mastering phpMyAdmin for Effective MySQL Management*" in April 2004 and subsequently continued to specialize in publishing highly focused books on specific technologies and solutions.

Our books and publications share the experiences of your fellow IT professionals in adapting and customizing today's systems, applications, and frameworks. Our solution-based books give you the knowledge and power to customize the software and technologies you're using to get the job done. Packt books are more specific and less general than the IT books you have seen in the past. Our unique business model allows us to bring you more focused information, giving you more of what you need to know, and less of what you don't.

Packt is a modern, yet unique publishing company, which focuses on producing quality, cutting-edge books for communities of developers, administrators, and newbies alike. For more information, please visit our website: www.PacktPub.com.

About Packt Enterprise

In 2010, Packt launched two new brands, Packt Enterprise and Packt Open Source, in order to continue its focus on specialization. This book is part of the Packt Enterprise brand, home to books published on enterprise software – software created by major vendors, including (but not limited to) IBM, Microsoft and Oracle, often for use in other corporations. Its titles will offer information relevant to a range of users of this software, including administrators, developers, architects, and end users.

Writing for Packt

We welcome all inquiries from people who are interested in authoring. Book proposals should be sent to author@packtpub.com. If your book idea is still at an early stage and you would like to discuss it first before writing a formal book proposal, contact us; one of our commissioning editors will get in touch with you.

We're not just looking for published authors; if you have strong technical skills but no writing experience, our experienced editors can help you develop a writing career, or simply get some additional reward for your expertise.

Microsoft System Center
2012 Orchestrator Cookbook

ISBN: 978-1-84968-850-5   Paperback: 318 pages

Automate mission-critical tasks with this practical, real-world guide to System Center 2012 Orchestrator

1. Create powerful runbooks for the System Center 2012 product line.

2. Master System Center 2012 Orchestrator by creating looping, child and branching runbooks.

3. Learn how to install System Center Orchestrator and make it secure and fault tolerant.

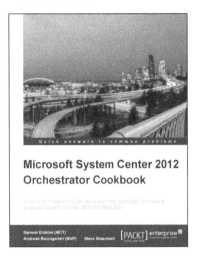

Microsoft System Center
Data Protection Manager
2012 SP1

ISBN: 978-1-84968-630-3   Paperback: 328 pages

Learn how to deploy, monitor, and administer System Center Data Protection Manager 2012 SP1

1. Practical guidance that will help you get the most out of Microsoft System Center Data Protection Manager 2012.

2. Gain insight into deploying, monitoring, and administering System Center Data Protection Manager 2012 from a team of Microsoft MVPs.

3. Learn the various methods and best practices for administrating and using Microsoft System Center Data Protection Manager 2012.

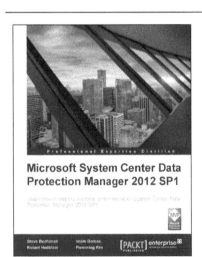

Please check **www.PacktPub.com** for information on our titles

Microsoft System Center Configuration Manager

ISBN: 978-1-78217-676-3   Paperback: 146 pages

Deploy a scalable solution by ensuring high availability and disaster recovery using Configuration Manager

1. Deploy highly available Configuration Manager sites and roles.

2. Back up, restore, and copy Configuration Manager to other sites.

3. Get to grips with performance tuning and best practices for Configuration Manager sites.

Microsoft System Center Virtual Machine Manager 2012 Cookbook

ISBN: 978-1-84968-632-7   Paperback: 342 pages

Over 60 recipes for the administration and management of Microsoft System Center Virtual Machine Manager 2012 SP1

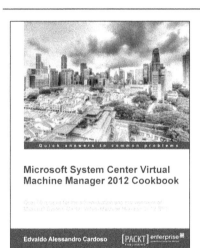

1. Create, deploy, and manage Datacenters and Private and Hybrid Clouds with hybrid hypervisors using VMM 2012 SP1, App Controller, and Operations Manager.

2. Integrate and manage fabric (compute, storages, gateways, and networking), services, and resources. Deploy Clusters from bare metal servers.

3. Learn how to use VMM 2012 SP1 features such as Windows 2012 and SQL 2012 support, Network Virtualization, Live Migration, Linux VMs, Resource Throttling, and Availability.

Please check **www.PacktPub.com** for information on our titles

www.ingramcontent.com/pod-product-compliance
Lightning Source LLC
Chambersburg PA
CBHW060525060326
40690CB00017B/3387